WHAT'S WRONG WITH OBAMAMANIA?

WHAT'S WRONG WITH OBAMAMANIA?

Black America, Black Leadership, and the Death of Political Imagination

RICKY L. JONES

With a foreword by

J. Blaine Hudson

STATE UNIVERSITY OF NEW YORK PRESS

Published by

STATE UNIVERSITY OF NEW YORK PRESS, ALBANY

© 2008 State University of New York

For information, contact State University of New York Press, Albany, NY
www.sunypress.edu

Production by Marilyn P. Semerad
Marketing by Susan M. Petrie

Library of Congress Cataloging-in-Publication Data

Jones, Ricky L.
  What's wrong with Obamamania? : Black America, Black leadership, and the death of political imagination / Ricky L. Jones.
    p. cm.
  Includes bibliographical references and index.
  ISBN 978-0-7914-7579-9 (hardcover : alk. paper)
  ISBN 978-0-7914-7580-5 (pbk. : alk. paper)
  1. Obama, Barack—Political and social views. 2. Obama, Barack—Public opinion.
3. Presidential candidates—United States. 4. African Americans—Politics and
government. 5. African American leadership. 6. African Americans—Social
conditions—1975– 7. Presidents—United States—Election—2008. 8. United States—
Race relations—Political aspects. 9. Political culture—United States. 10. Public
opinion—United States. I. Title.

E901.1.O23J66 2008
973'.0496073—dc22
                                                                2007049896

10   9   8   7   6   5   4   3   2

Once again, for Linnie Mae Jones—my grandmother, warrior, and cancer survivor. Also, for her oncologist, Dr. Jonathan Kaufman of Emory University, who has worked diligently in helping her continue to live a bold and adventurous life. Fight on, Mama!

Also for James R. Terry, J. Blaine Hudson, Robert Douglas, and Chester Grundy—outstanding educators and men of depth and sacrifice. You are the finest examples of leadership I have known. You have all inspired me to be a better man.

Contents

Another thing that we must do in speeding up the coming of the new age is to develop intelligent, courageous, and dedicated leadership. This is one of the pressing needs of the hour. In this period of transition and growing social change, there is a dire need for leaders who are calm and yet positive; leaders who avoid the extremes of "hotheadedness" and "Uncle Tomism." The urgency of the hour calls for leaders of wise judgment and sound integrity: leaders not in love with money but in love with justice; leaders not in love with publicity, but in love with humanity; leaders who can subject their particular egos to the greatness of the cause. To paraphrase Holland's words: God give us leaders!

> A time like this demands strong minds, great hearts, true faith
>   and ready hands;
> Leaders whom the lust of office does not kill;
> Leaders whom the spoils of life cannot buy;
> Leaders who possess opinions and a will;
> Leaders who have honor; leaders who will not lie;
> Leaders who can stand before a demagogue and damn his
>   treacherous flatteries without winking!
> Tall leaders, sun crowned, who live above the fog in public
>   duty and private thinking.
>
> —Martin Luther King Jr., "Facing the Challenge of a
> New Age," Montgomery, Alabama (December 3, 1956)

Foreword

Readers attracted to catchy titles will probably be caught by this one, *What's Wrong with Obamamania?* and may expect yet another version of Rush Limbaugh's *Barack the Magic Negro*, suitable for sale at local supermarkets or Wal-Mart. Fortunately, if they read beyond the title and their own assumptions, they will be pleasantly surprised and may find that the question has no simple answer and serves only as a point of departure for a far-ranging, insightful, and illuminating analysis of black political leadership over time. In Dr. Ricky Jones' extremely capable hands, this rather facetious question becomes a window into the American racial past, present, and perhaps, future—a window through which we can see much that we need, but seldom wish, to see clearly.

Asking "What's wrong with Obamamania?" also poses the question, "What's wrong with Barack Obama?"—and for that matter, "What's right with Barack Obama?" They all prompt a few other queries far more fundamental to our understanding of race in this country. For example, Why is it so unusual to consider Barack Obama a serious contender for the office of president of the United States—rather than another African American making a largely symbolic run for the White House? Clearly, as the only sitting black United States senator, he is an intelligent, articulate, and capable politician. As a man of African ancestry, he is exotic but not "ethnic" in a pejorative sense. He neither rejects nor expresses ambivalence about his blackness as, for example, Michael Jackson and Tiger Woods have done. However, while he conforms neither to the popular stereotype of black males of the hip-hop generation nor to the older image of the black civil rights leader, he does conform to another stereotype embedded as deeply in American culture. In other words, if the image of the black male of gangsta rap is the modern incarnation of the "black buck" or the "coon," Barack Obama, in the minds of many Americans, is the modern incarnation of the "faithful black servant"—the new "corporate" black man whose purpose in life and relatively privileged place in the world are determined solely by his usefulness to privileged whites.[1]

Of course, there is a deep and fatal flaw in both the new and old versions of this stereotype. The "faithful black servant" is not and never can be his own master or her own mistress. White Americans have never been so trusting or so foolish as to give such servants the kind of real power and autonomy that would equip them to pursue a truly independent agenda, particularly as relates to race. However, as the past few generations have shown, white America *has* been willing to allow a few such useful black individuals to rise to unprecedented heights—as long as they were content to serve or preserve the interests of privileged white Americans. The list of examples is long indeed—stretching from Jackie Robinson and Ralph Bunche two generations ago to Condoleezza Rice and Clarence Thomas today, and including a host of highly paid athletes, business executives, educational administrators, public intellectuals, and entrepreneurs who prosper in a political economy over which they have no real control but in which they all, whether they or others always know it or not, fill roles that make them valuable to privileged white Americans—and conversely, disposable when they are no longer valuable.

This is not an impossible dilemma, but it is, I believe, a difficult one that bears directly on where Barack Obama "fits" in contemporary America. The post–civil rights era ended with the disputed election of President George W. Bush in 2000 and the tragedy of September 11, 2001. Although this new era has not yet been named, it dawned with the fateful intersection of a reactionary presidential administration and a national tragedy that allowed that conservative faction to seize unprecedented power and then to act nationally and globally to advance its ideological and economic interests under the guise of preserving American security. While we can only speculate about the long-term consequences of offensive wars in Afghanistan and Iraq, and U.S. global policies in general, the immediate consequences for black America and for persons of color throughout the world are becoming increasingly clear.

In this country, for example, between 2000 and 2004, the average American family lost 3.6 percent of its median income, with white Americans losing 2.1 percent, Asian and Hispanic Americans losing roughly 6.0 percent and African Americans losing 7.4 percent.[2] In other words, between Bush tax and economic policies and the economic downturn since 9/11, the gains of the Clinton era (which recouped the losses of the Reagan and Bush (I) eras) were wiped out, literally, over night. Put in perspective, even before the disastrous slippage of the past few years, African American family income was barely 60 percent of white American family income, and, thus, the glacial process of reducing structural inequality by race was halted and reversed again, as it was a generation ago after the election of Ronald Reagan.

These gross national trends mask an even more insidious and ominous shift—the growing distance between the "haves" and "have-nots," that is, the "hollowing-out" of societies around the world as the middle-class shrinks, the "haves" become "have-mores," and the "have-nots" grow more numerous and more marginal. For example, the Gini index (developed by Italian statistician Corrado Gini in 1912), which measures income inequality by comparing the total income of the poorest 20 percent of a nation's population with the total income of the richest 20 percent (on a scale of 0 to 100, with 100 representing perfect inequality) is growing in most nations. At one extreme, poor nations with small groups of wealthy people have always produced high Gini coefficients. For example, Sierra Leone has a Gini coefficient of 62.9. Wealthier nations with large poor (often distinguishable by racial and color differences) populations also have high coefficients. For example, Brazil has a Gini coefficient of 60.7, South Africa 59.3. At the other extreme, nations with large middle-class populations report much lower coefficients, such as Hungary at 24.4, Japan at 24.9. Since September 11, the United States has "slipped" quietly from the 30s into the 40s on the Gini index.[3] And, if the middle class is shrinking generally, the black middle class—already smaller numerically and proportionally, and already weaker in terms of actual wealth compared to the white middle class—is eroding even more rapidly despite the spectacular achievements of a few moguls, athletes, entertainers, and entrepreneurs.

Given the facts of the present and the facts of history, the "place" of African Americans in contemporary American society, once stripped of familiar and useful illusions, best fits the "fourth world" or "internal colonial" paradigm developed conceptually, if not by name, by a succession of black intellectuals in recent decades.[4] The explanatory power of this paradigm is equaled only by the degree of discomfort it causes most Americans, including most black Americans. That power is undeniable when applied to the plight of the masses of African Americans isolated by both race and poverty. However, accounting for the plight of more privileged African Americans such as Barack Obama—who owe, in most cases, their relatively privileged status to their roles in the larger, still white-controlled society—is more troublesome and more difficult.

For example, African Americans expect and insist upon a level of racial representation in all walks of American life as a simple litmus test of fundamental fairness, as a measure of progress toward equality or the lack thereof. Yet, all too often, African Americans also feel profoundly ambivalent toward the men and women who occupy those roles. Is it desirable or not, good or bad, to have a black chief of police, college professor or president, school superintendent, entrepreneur, movie star, public intellectual, or judge or elected official such as Barack Obama? How often are individuals who cross the invisible border into the larger society thought to have crossed into the "white world"? And, if so, how often are they considered representatives or an intellectual vanguard or warriors seeking to advance the interests of those left behind? And how often as "sell-outs"?

Yet these same individuals, and usually as isolated individuals, must traffic daily with a world in which racism remains virulent and in which they are almost always a small minority, and, of course, the more privileged the role, the smaller a minority they are likely to be. Even if they have the appearance of power, it is all too often borrowed or derivative in a larger corporate or institutional structure. Even if they have the trappings of wealth, they control neither the political nor the economic system that makes that wealth possible and regulates how it can be held and expended. Thus, as the segments of black America on either side of the race/class divide drift farther apart, the existential reality of life in the "mainstream" for those, such as Barack Obama, attempting to navigate its straits and rapids is very different from what those trapped outside the mainstream may perceive it to be.

Still, as we elaborate the paradigm somewhat, an internal colony is only coincidentally a "place" or a network of "places" but is essentially a relationship between groups different racially and unequal in power and wealth. Such relationships exist in the "fourth world," that is, the social and political space occupied by one or more racial minority groups in societies dominated by a different racial majority group. In objective terms, internal colonies may become "reservations" or Bantustans that afford the illusion of autonomy but cannot become autonomous economic or political units in the bosoms of their home societies.

Of course, there are both limitations and possibilities inherent in being so situated. On the one hand, fourth-world groups can never achieve the degree of independence and power possible in the black majority countries of the so-called third world. On the other hand, fourth-world groups are usually at the "bottom" of the world's wealthiest societies—a plight often far better than being in the "middle" or even at the "top" of the world's poorest nations. The point, of course, is simple and telling: given such limitations, those who would "move up" must also "move out" to some degree, if no farther than to a segregated black middle-class enclave. In other words, the familiar alternatives that populate a host of ideological fantasies and debates are perfectly fine for late-night musings and hair-splitting in journals, conferences, and political meetings, but they have done "no work in the real world," so to speak, because they are inherently unworkable under fourth-world or internal colonial conditions.

For more privileged African Americans, the means of escaping the trap of being no more than a "good servant" or a contemporary "house Negro" or, in fourth-world terms, a member of the "native elite," must transcend the superficial identification with "being black" or occasional spasms of "speaking truth to power" (usually for a fee). Rather, these individuals, beyond whatever is required for their own careers and the maintenance of their own families, must be willing to form networks or more formal organizations, and/or simply to act outside the bounds of "good business" or narrow self-interest to further the "freedom agenda" of the twenty-first century—to act not only on their own behalf but on behalf of those left out and left behind, and, by so doing, keep faith with the tradition of black struggle and leadership in this country stretching back to Richard Allen, David Walker, Frances Ellen Watkins Harper, Frederick Douglass, and so many others. These are not class traitors or "spooks who sit by the door." These are simply men and women who understand implicitly that, in the fourth world, in the haunting and largely forgotten words of Harry Belafonte in the motion picture *Island in the Sun* (1957): "My skin is my country."

Only in this way can powerless individuals create power as groups: by pooling the surplus value of their talents, time, and treasure to serve the larger ends of black America and, ultimately, the cause of human freedom, justice, and equality. This course of action may mean taking risks and making sacrifices, but, as W. E. B. Du Bois stated nearly eighty years ago, the more people are willing to share the risk, the less risk to any individual.[5] For me, then, the real issue underlying the question, "What's wrong with Obamamania?" is not whether Barack Obama is or is not "authentically black," when the meaning of being "authentically black" is contested and fluid, but whether Barack Obama is committed to this freedom agenda, that is, has he done, is he doing, will he do anything tangible to help real, not abstract, African Americans and to contribute to the achievement, in measurable, objective terms, of greater pluralism and racial equality in this society and around the world?[6] What remains to be seen, of course, is whether Barack Obama can serve this agenda and still be sufficiently safe and useful to remain a credible presidential candidate.

In the following pages, Ricky L. Jones combines the passion and commitment of a social activist with the knowledge and skills of a seasoned scholar to examine not only Barack Obama, but to trace the evolution of this "freedom agenda" and how African Americans and our allies have carried it forward over time, or sometimes failed to do so, and why. Clearly, the value of his work far transcends the presidential election of 2008 as well as those that will follow.

J. Blaine Hudson

Jesse Jackson Didn't Give a Damn!

Ain't nobody fighting, 'cause nobody knows what to say.
—Gil Scott-Heron, "Winter in America"

A leader is a dealer in hope.
—Napoleon Bonaparte

I am a worrier. Let me give you an example. A few months ago, while driving home from work I had a troubling experience. It was a nice spring day—nothing unusual. As I sat at a traffic signal listening to music, I noticed a black woman walking past my car. She seemed to be in her mid to late forties—mocha skinned with a slender build. Maybe she was making her way home from a hard day's work. She was certainly laboring. She was struggling not just because of the toils of the day, but also because she was dealing with some type of debilitating condition— maybe multiple sclerosis or something else. I really do not know. Her right arm and hand were bent and she arduously pulled one of her legs along as she moved.

As I witnessed the awesome sight of this woman in all her glory, I turned my music down and almost shed a tear. I do not know what it was about her. Maybe her build and skin tone reminded me of my mother, who has battled drug addiction for as long as I can remember. Maybe she reminded me of the many black women in the Atlanta projects where I grew up—catching the bus early and returning to our poverty-stricken, walled-in community late, exhausted. It was a daily struggle for them, too, just trying to make ends meet. Who knows what struck me. A horn honked behind me and snapped me out of my daze. "Move along," they insisted. I complied and left the woman behind. I was proud of her, this queen—walking, dragging, enduring. To be sure, with every step she toiled, but as my fellow motorists had prompted me to do, she was moving forward. She seemed to do it without complaint, without self-pity. I wondered what her story was. How did she come to be this way? What was her life like? Was she really coming from work? Would she be all right? I worried about her. It was not the first time I had worried. You see, I am black, and I worry about my people. It has been this way for some time.

A few years before I saw that woman who still lingers in my memory, my worrying brought me to, of all places, a church on Easter Sunday. There I sat among a small group of "trouble-makers" counter-protesting a Jesse Jackson–led march against police brutality. "Protest Jesse?" you might ask. "That's strange. Shouldn't Jesse be doing the protesting?" It most certainly was strange. The whole scene was weird for a number of reasons. It was not unusual to see a black person in church on Easter Sunday, but it was out of the ordinary to see me in church on *any* Sunday. You see, I had stopped attending years earlier. The only times I showed up now were Mother's Day and New Year's Watch Night Service for the sake of my grandmother who had been a devout member of the Church of God in Christ for as long as I could remember.

I do not want to be misunderstood. I did not stop going to church because I stopped believing in God. I stopped going because I stopped believing in the black church. I grew tired of the entertainment without education; perpetual fund-raising without demonstrable betterment in the lives of the people giving the funds; gaudy, hustling, increasingly wealthy, professional preachers and financially strapped flocks; voices from the pulpits and the pews screaming for all the wrong reasons. I just got tired of it all. As a result, I left church alone. But, here I was—in a church (the starting point for the march) along with a few other "believers," about to "protest a protest" led by Jackson and some of the most powerful ministers, business people, and politicians in Louisville's black community. What an ugly scene this was to become. How did it all come to this? In my early thirties, I was still a bit young and, admittedly, naive. I knew what we were about to do would not change the world, but I sure did think it would change Louisville. I was wrong of course, but what would youth be without dreams?

On its face, the protest march was noble. It was a response to a number of major issues. Heading the list was the ever-present police brutality plaguing African Americans in Louisville and beyond. The headliner case was Adrian Reynolds. Reynolds initially made news after he was beaten by police during a January 1998 arrest for hitting his girlfriend during a domestic dispute. After an internal investigation, no disciplinary action was recommended for any of the officers involved. Six days after his arrest, Reynolds died of a head injury sustained during a scuffle with corrections officers at the Jefferson County Jail. One officer was charged with murder but was ultimately acquitted.

In May 1999, Desmond Rudolph was fatally shot by police as he attempted to free a stolen vehicle stuck in a western Louisville alley. A grand jury cleared the officers based on evidence supporting their account that Rudolph had freed the truck, and the officers feared they would be run over. In response to these cases, Jesse Jackson, the last heavy-hitter of the civil rights movement was called in. Jackson leading what was called the "March toward Destiny" would be the culminating event of his visit. The old King protégé's stopover in Louisville along with the march were heralded as a sea change. Some of us were not so sure.

One of Jackson's first moves was to enlist the support of the ministers of Louisville's largest churches. He also sat at the heart of a decision to have the march end at one of the minister's church properties. The problem was these ministers were not committed to the march or the cause. In fact, most had either taken very politically conservative stances or had been strangely silent on the issues in question. On the Desmond Rudolph case, in fact, one minister had repeatedly commented that Rudolph would be alive if he had not been involved in an illegal lifestyle. While the pastor's stance held some argumentative merit, it certainly seemed contradictory that he would be involved in the leadership of a march protesting Rudolph's shooting. Some of us immediately set upon a letter-writing campaign to Jesse Jackson to make that and other points.

We stressed to Jackson that we were "no less than appalled at the arrival of the [ministers] at the eleventh hour." Not only had they emerged late, but they were subsequently perceived by many as the leadership of an already existing movement. This development was disturbing to say the least. To whom would the people turn after Jackson left? Clearly, these men were recruited because their involvement would prompt the support of their relatively large flocks for the march. However, we were not sure if Jackson was aware of the disturbingly conservative sociopolitical stances the ministers had taken in previous years. What the city needed was strong, committed leadership. It did not need to be sacrosanct, but sincere, trusted, and accountable to the people. To the contrary, these men were among a group of clergy that had engaged in actions that led many to believe they were prone to forming alliances with the very power brokers who supported initiatives that marginalized poor people and people of color locally and nationally. In fact, later that same year Jackson returned to Louisville and openly chided members of this same group for potentially damaging Eleanor Jordan's candidacy for Congress by tying themselves to conservative Republican Congresswoman Anne Northup.

Jackson said his fellow ministers should not "forfeit the historic possibility of electing a black woman to Congress (which had never been done in Kentucky) in return for a mess of pottage." A week before the November 2000 elections, one minister who had received grant money from Northup, supported her by attending a Republican campaign rally, and refuted Jackson by commenting to the local newspaper, "I don't consider it pottage, I consider it a return of tax dollars to the total community that we've never seen at this level." Of course, Louisville was reflective of many cities in America—plagued by abnormally weak black political leadership and disproportionately strong religious control. The preachers filled a yawning void created by apathy, cynicism, and fear, and they used these factors to their benefit.

Jackson never responded to our letters. Maybe he was trapped in a place most people are, comfortable with familiarity, even if the familiar is bad. Maybe he was just replicating what he had done hundreds of times before: wait for a crisis situation, enlist the support of the city's most powerful ministers (whether they were sincerely committed to the cause or not), do a little publicity, swing into the city by late morning, lead a march, deliver words of condemnation and encouragement, and fly back out that evening, leaving the city in the hands of men he had empowered with ministerial photo ops. Somewhere in this, of course, he would take the opportunity to raise a bit of money for Rainbow/PUSH. That fact should not be ignored. But maybe Jackson was authentic. Maybe he really cared and was just doing what he thought was best. From where I was sitting, that was not the case. From where I was sitting, Jesse Jackson didn't give a damn. He was just reading from an old and rather tired script. Frankly, I have not felt the same about him since.

After Jackson left Louisville in the midst of controversy after our "protest of the protest" the city returned to business as usual. The drum of death continued to beat. Mentally impaired Rodney Abernathy was fatally shot by police in June 2000 during an altercation that began with Abernathy hitting himself in the head with a jack handle. Police said Abernathy charged them. A grand jury decided not to indict any of the officers. Clifford Lewis was fatally shot in January 2001 after the van he was driving pinned a police officer between the van and another vehicle, injuring his leg and foot. Police said the detective who fired the shots thought his life was in danger. Antwan Bryant was fatally shot in February 2001 while riding in the back seat of a vehicle that backed over a police officer's legs. In December 2002, fifty-year-old James Taylor (with his hands cuffed behind his back) was shot eleven times by police and killed. Officers claimed that, despite his bondage, somehow Taylor was able to lunge at them with a box-cutter. Louisville was not alone.

In April 2003, a twenty-six-year-old mother of two, Charquisa Johnson, was shot and killed by Washington, D.C., police. Contrary to police reports, eyewitnesses said she was unarmed with hands in the air when she was gunned down. In May, unarmed Ousmane Zongo was shot and killed by New York City police in a botched raid in a Manhattan warehouse. Five days later, a New York medical examiner ruled the death of Alberta Spruill, a fifty-seven-year-old black grandmother, a homicide and said police officers were directly responsible for causing her heart attack because they raided her apartment based on bad information from an informant. In June, twenty-eight-year-old Terrence Shurn was killed when his motorcycle crashed while being chased by police in Benton Harbor, Michigan. His death set off several nights of fires and "riots." Shurn's crime? Driving with a suspended license. Four days later, yet another young, unarmed black man was shot and killed by police in south Philadelphia.

In many of these places, Jackson or a Jacksonlike figure showed up, and black people followed them. Even after it was revealed that Jackson fathered a child out of wedlock, black people continued to follow. Such behavior was not new. They also continued to support Marion Barry after he was caught smoking crack in the late 1980s. A good percentage even supported Clarence Thomas when he fought for confirmation to the Supreme Court. Some of the choices seemed strange to say the least. I wondered why. The answer was actually very simple. It was simple and sad. Jackson and the others, to different degrees of course, represented something black folks always needed more of. It was more than Jesse's patented "keep hope alive" mantra. For brief moments in time, when he stood before them, black people really believed something could be changed. They really believed someone could save them. At least they *wanted* to believe it. Jackson and every burgeoning local black activist, politician, and preacher across the country represented externally what so many did not have internally: hope.

In 2004, another man (like Jackson, also based in Chicago) burst onto the scene and tickled the country's long-dormant political imagination. He reignited Americans' capacity to believe, to dream—to hope.

He emerged like a breath of fresh air on a crisp fall morning. He seemed to be a politician who did not succumb to the pettiness of politics; a black man who was not limited by the constraints of race; a Democrat who just might have a few new ideas. Of course, none of us knew what those ideas were. In fact, few people really seemed to care. All most people occupied themselves with was the idea that this man somehow appeared to be "different." His name was Barack Hussein Obama Jr.

Obama stepped boldly onto the national scene in the summer of 2004 with a now almost mythic speech at the Democratic National Convention. Overnight, he catapulted into the stratosphere of political and pop-culture superstardom. He was an interesting figure during interesting times. Born in 1961, Obama belongs to one of the first generations of Americans that has no prolonged firsthand experience with slavery or legal segregation. This has consequences that extend well beyond any single individual. Not only has American society made many profound shifts over the years, but black American leadership has also radically changed since the modern civil rights movement ended with Martin Luther King Jr.'s death in 1968. For good or ill, the alterations are deep seated and far reaching.

By the time most Americans figured out who Barack Obama was, King had been dead for more than three and a half decades. His dual roles in black America have been splintered. The activist King has been replaced by men such as Jesse Jackson and Al Sharpton. King's ministerial shoes now warm the feet of the T. D. Jakes and Creflo Dollars of the world. Andrew Young, born out of a revolutionary, progressive tradition, once epitomized America's highest-ranking government officials. In the new order, Republican loyalists Colin Powell and Condoleezza Rice hold that honor. Talented athletes with a sociopolitical conscience such as Paul Robeson, Jim Brown, and Muhammad Ali have given way to the likes of Michael Jordan, who seems more interested in selling sneakers than justice.

The most popular black politicians look nothing like the firebrand Adam Clayton Powell Jr. Now, moderate to conservative legislators such as Harold Ford Jr. are considered the up-and-comers. Thurgood Marshall no longer holds fellow Supreme Court justices' feet to the fire. Clarence Thomas now sits in his chair. The message music of Curtis Mayfield, Gil Scott-Heron, James Brown, and the Last Poets is gone. It has been replaced by the aggressive, depoliticized street operas of Lil' Wayne, Young Jeezy, the Ying Yang Twins and T. I. More important, the dominant form of black music is no longer a soundtrack to a sociopolitical movement at all. Hip-hop is now a movement in and of itself.

Individually, William Edward Burghardt Du Bois' idea of educated blacks serving as leaders of the race with the best interests of the masses at heart has given way to a predominantly elitist vulgar careerist ethic that does little to connect to the poor. Collectively, the tradition of well-heeled blacks standing in solidarity with the less privileged reaching far back as the 1830s with the National Negro Convention movement is gone. A new black petit and aspiring bourgeoisie ruled by greed, excess, and apoliticism now plagues us. Our current substitutes for the radical agenda of *Crisis* magazine are the shallowness of *Ebony* and *Essence* and the debauchery of Black Entertainment Television. Small community-committed businessmen and women such as A. G. Gaston and Mary Ann Shadd Cary have faded from the scene. In their places stand national and international moguls such as Oprah Winfrey, Russell Simmons, and Robert Johnson.

This is our new world—the new landscape of black America. It is less progressive, more nihilistic and numb. In many respects, it is closer to a post–civil rights nightmare than King's dream. Black leadership in this new reality has definitely expanded in quantity, but its quality and commitment trouble many. We cannot deny that we have serious problems—some old and persistent, others new and equally incorrigible. To place the entire responsibility for solving the problems of black America on the shoulders of Barack Obama would be unfair and foolish. To blame him for the dilemmas we continue to face would be even more ludicrous. Obama did not create black America's current reality. Like all of us, he is a product of it. But there is a pressing question before us: Are Obama and the new brand of black leadership a part of the problem, the solution, or both? There is no easy black-and-white (no pun intended) answer to that query, but the pages that follow seek to prompt a bit of thought on the subject.

No matter what conclusions we draw, Obama's future seems bright. While he mulled over whether or not to run for president in 2008, Jesse Jackson weighed in and promised his support. Jackson, who campaigned for president in 1984 and 1988, told CNN he was all but certain to endorse Obama if he decided to run. "All of my heart leans toward Barack," Jackson said. "He is a next-door neighbor literally. I think he's an extension of our struggle to make this a more perfect union." As for me, I am still a bit worried.

1

A Series of Unfortunate (and Unsavory) Events

Paving the Way for "Obamamania"

> It's like when you go to the dentist, and the man's going to
> take your tooth. You're going to fight him when he starts
> pulling. So he squirts some stuff in your jaw called Novo-
> cain, to make you think they're not doing anything to you.
> So you sit there and, because you've got all of that Novo-
> cain in your jaw, you suffer peacefully. Blood running all
> down your jaw, and you don't know what's happening
> because someone has taught you to suffer—peacefully.
> —Malcolm X, *Message to the Grassroots*

L ike all of us, Barack Obama exists in a world where certain groups
suffer disproportionately. As with all downtrodden people, an ever-
present question looms for America's poor and colored: What's next?
Less than a year after Obama's election to the United States Senate,
another in a long series of answers presented itself. This time her name
was Katrina. In the wake of the unimaginable destruction caused by
Hurricane Katrina in 2005, many Americans called for a new national
discussion on race, racism, and class. From jazz impresario Wynton
Marsalis' thoughtful article in *Time* to a plethora of missives from black
intellectuals, various voices posited that the ugly reality of systemic
American racial dichotomization still demanded attention.[1] Unfortunately, they were largely dismissed in the main.

The lion's share of white Americans proclaimed there was no racial
dynamic involved in government response or anything else in the Gulf

Coast region following Katrina's devastation. This was simply a natural disaster, and natural disasters made no choices based on race. Of course, this was true: the storm made no conscious decisions. But had our country made choices long before Katrina that diminished certain citizens' life chances because of the color of their skin? The debate was intense. Just as Katrina's rain and winds faded into history, former Reagan secretary of education and George H. Bush drug czar William Bennett asserted on his nationally syndicated radio show, "I do know that it's true that if you wanted to reduce crime, you could—if that were your sole purpose, you could abort every black baby in this country, and your crime rate would go down." He quickly added, "That would be an impossible, ridiculous and morally reprehensible thing to do, but your crime rate would go down."[2]

While some called Bennett's comments offensive and racist, he was not without supporters. Rush Limbaugh opined that Bennett "should have been applauded" for his comment. National Review columnist Andrew McCarthy called Bennett's statement "a minor point that was statistically and logically unassailable."[3] McCarthy was incensed by what he called "a shameful effort to paint him [Bennett] as a racist. He's about as bigoted as Santa Claus." Courtland Milloy of the Washington Post (who is black) flipped the issue back onto black folk when he argued that black people really had no right to be upset about Bennett's comment, because many of them are actually engaging in the abortion process. "There is a problem here," Milloy chided, "but it's not Bennett, whose comments illuminated a moral inconsistency in black America that is far more harmful than anything he said."[4] As a consequence of either denial, ignorance, or deception, these fellows missed the point. Why was Bennett immediately drawn to the example of black babies? Why not Asian, Hispanic, Jewish or even white ones?

Before the Bennett coffee brewed, three white New Orleans police officers mercilessly beat sixty-four-year-old retired black elementary school teacher Robert Davis in the French Quarter. Like Rodney King and Donovan Jackson-Chavis, the thrashing was caught on tape, but, of course, nothing wrong or racial really happened. The officers claimed they merely had to restrain Davis because he was publicly intoxicated and resisted arrest. Contrarily, Davis stated he had not had a drink in twenty-five years. Interestingly, no breathalyzer was taken. As in many cases of black men being beaten or killed by police across the country, New Orleans Police spokesperson Marlon Defillo said "race was not an issue."[5] Officer Robert Evangelist was charged in the beating but ultimately acquitted by District Judge Frank Murillo in a trial without a jury in July 2007. Murillo commented after the trial that he "didn't even find [the case] a close call."

The denial of a racial dynamic is often a reality in cases such as these because, for many, the end of racial history (and the racism that accompanied it) is upon us. If one defines race out of existence (ala Ward Conerly) or denies the reality of racism, neither requires engagement. At this historical moment, across lines of race, many deny the persistence of racism and its often violent physical, psychological, and public policy consequences. To make matters worse, those who seek to call attention to these issues are often themselves labeled racist. Barack Obama does not have this problem.

No one has accused Obama of racial bias, because he has not talked much about race since arriving on the national scene. For many, the fact that he avoids any deep analysis of the subject is a part of his appeal. For others, that reluctance raises a great deal of angst. Outside of the pesky race issue, what else (if anything) is wrong with Barack Obama? One of my colleagues at the University of Louisville joked, "His name sounds too much like Osama" (one would suppose the middle name Hussein would also give a few xenophobes pause). Beyond that, at first glance Obama seems almost flawless. To be sure, he is nothing short of the greatest political phenomenon in recent memory. He is tall, handsome, of exotic racial heritage (his father Kenyan, mother white American), clearly intelligent, masterful with words, and charismatic. Obama is only the fifth black U.S. senator in the history of the country—only the third since Reconstruction. He even won a Grammy for the spoken word version of his autobiography. He is easily the Democrats' hottest commodity. To be sure, this is not difficult. Even though the Republicans have accumulated a veritable laundry list of missteps that many think have placed the country and world at risk, both the 2006 midterms and 2008 presidential year elections were and are, respectively, in doubt.

Wrong Turns for the Right

As the country prepared for the 2006 midterms, the list of Republican embarrassments was long, both professionally and personally. Political careers started to take hits in 2005 surrounding the indictment and eventual conviction of lobbyist Jack Abramoff of numerous improprieties. The first to fall was California House member Randy "Duke" Cunningham, an associate of Abramoff, who resigned from the House in November 2005 after pleading guilty to accepting at least $2.4 million in bribes and underreporting his income for 2004. He pleaded guilty to federal charges of conspiracy to commit bribery, mail fraud, wire fraud, and tax evasion. In March 2006, he received a sentence of eight years and four months in prison and an order to pay $1.8 million in restitution.

In June 2006, longtime Republican enforcer and House majority leader Tom DeLay, also associated with Abramoff, resigned his Texas seat to fight charges that he illegally funneled corporate funds to state legislative races. DeLay denied wrongdoing, but two of his former aides pleaded guilty in the Abramoff case. In July 2006, uber-conservative Ralph Reed, of Christian Coalition fame and a former Abramoff friend and associate, lost a primary race for lieutenant governor in Georgia. Of course, any number of factors not involving Abramoff could have contributed to Reed's loss. The same could not be said for Ohio Republican Bob Ney. In May 2006, the House Ethics Committee launched an investigation into bribery charges against Ney. In August, he announced he would not run for a seventh House term. At the time of his resignation, the Justice Department was also investigating allegations that Ney took gifts, trips, and campaign donations from Abramoff and his clients in exchange for official actions. Like DeLay, Ney denied wrongdoing and said he decided not to run in an effort to spare his family. "I can no longer put them through this ordeal," he said.[6]

In August 2006, while campaigning for reelection to the United States Senate, then Republican presidential hopeful George Allen seemed to cross the line with a racial insult. During a campaign rally in Breaks, Virginia, Allen pointed out S. R. Sidarth, an Indian American volunteer from the camp of opponent James Webb. Sidarth, a twenty-year-old University of Virginia student, was serving as reconnaissance for Webb with the common political practice of taping Allen's rallies and looking for chinks in his armor. Before a totally white audience (not including Sidarth), Allen launched into a brief but troubling rant. "This fellow here. Over here with the yellow shirt, Macaca, or whatever his name is. He's with my opponent. He's following us around everywhere. And it's just great," Allen said, as his supporters began to laugh. After noting that Webb was raising money in California with a "bunch of Hollywood movie moguls," Allen said, "Let's give a welcome to Macaca here. Welcome to America and the real world of Virginia." Despite the sarcastic "welcome," Sidarth was already at home. He was actually born in Virginia. Ironically, Allen was the outsider of sorts. He was born in, of all places, California.

As it turns out, "macaca" or "macaque" (literally a type of monkey) is a rather nasty racial slur originally used by Francophone colonials when referring to native populations of North and Sub-Saharan Africa. In *The Troubled Heart in Africa*, Robert Edgerton recounts that in the Belgian Congo colonial whites called Africans "*macaques*" and insisted that they had only recently come down from trees. The term *sale macaque* (filthy monkey) was also occasionally used.[7] The word is still used in Belgium as a racial slur referring to Moroccan immigrants or their descendants. Among other things, Allen's camp and his supporters claimed he did not even know what "macaca" meant, and he simply "made the word up."

Beyond that, Allen asserted that he was just teasing Sidarth. Further investigation prompted some to believe that maybe Allen *did* know the word's meaning. At a University of Virginia commencement ceremony in 2005, the wife of his collegiate French professor who introduced Allen bragged that Allen's performance in French was "excellent." The plot thickened when Allen's parentage was examined. In Tunisia, "macaca" is used as a racial pejorative when referring to black Africans, similar to the way "nigger" is used is the United States. By Allen's own admission, his mother is a French colonial born in Tunisia. So there was at least the possibility he had been exposed to the word "macaca."

Disturbingly, conservative advocates rarely apologize for such offenses. They either seek to explain them away or divert attention from the issue. In the Allen case, conservative columnist Cal Thomas attacked former King protégé Andrew Young rather than unconditionally condemn Allen. Thomas asserted that Young's comments about some Jews, Koreans, and Arabs who operated businesses in black neighborhoods were more racist (if such a thing can be measured) than Allen calling Sidarth a monkey.[8]

To be fair, Young sank himself into hot water with no help from Thomas. In August 2006, the *Los Angeles Sentinel* asked Young about serving as a Wal-Mart spokesman even though the chain forced a number of mom-and-pop stores out of business. Young commented,

> Well, I think they should; they ran the mom-and-pop stores out of my neighborhood. But you see, these are the people who have been overcharging us, selling us stale bread and bad meat and wilted vegetables. And they sold out and moved to Florida. I think they've ripped off our communities enough. First it was Jews, then it was Koreans and now its Arabs; very few black people own these stores.[9]

At the time Young was heading Working Families for Wal-Mart, a group whose mission was to help improve the retail and corporate giant's public image in minority neighborhoods. To be sure, Young (like many, not all, of the old civil rights icons) was baring his capitalist fangs—this time for Wal-Mart. This fact should not be ignored even though he resigned in the midst of the controversy because, in his words, he "didn't want to become a distraction from the main issues."

Thomas's skewering of Young aside, Virginia voters initially seemed largely unmoved by Allen's "macaca moment" or subsequent defenses. Following the insults and denials, Allen remained the front-runner for some time before his eventual loss to Webb by a slim margin. In fact, the Allen debacle was not the first public display of racial insensitivity from a Grand Old Party heavyweight in recent memory. One of the most notable was probably Trent Lott's now infamous speech at Strom Thurmond's one hundredth birthday party and retirement celebration, which eventually led to the Mississippi senator stepping down from his position as Senate minority leader in 2002 (Lott held his Senate seat until his retirement in late 2007. He was named minority whip in 2006).

In 1948, when the Democratic Party nominated Harry Truman for president on a platform featuring a prominent civil rights plank, Thurmond proclaimed that Truman's federal antilynching and antipoll tax initiatives were "oppressive" to southern states and threatened to destroy the South's "way of life." Thurmond, who some argue reformed later in life, famously exclaimed, "All the laws of Washington and all the bayonets of the Army cannot force the Nigger race into our homes, our schools, our churches." In support of this stance, disgruntled white southern "Dixiecrats," led by the Mississippi delegation, left the Democratic Convention and organized a separate States' Rights Party that nominated Thurmond for president and Mississippi governor Fielding Wright as his running mate. Despite Truman's reelection, the Dixiecrat ticket carried four states from the Deep South: Alabama, Louisiana, South Carolina, and Mississippi. Mississippi gave the Dixiecrats 87 percent of its vote.

Alluding to this fact, Lott exclaimed, "I want to say this about my state: When Strom Thurmond ran for president, we voted for him. We're proud of it. And if the rest of the country had followed our lead, we wouldn't have had all these problems over all these years, either."[10] Strangely, Lott labeled Thurmond "a great humanitarian" despite the fact that many regard him as the epitome of the most virulent forms of racism and white supremacy in American politics and society in the twentieth century.

To cap the GOP's troubles off just before the 2006 midterms, Florida Republican congressman and House deputy whip Mark Foley resigned in late September after a series of sexually explicit e-mails sent to teenage male pages surfaced. In one note from August 2005, Foley asked a sixteen-year-old page if he made him "a little horny." According to ABC News, some of the exchanges were too graphic to be made public.[11] After his resignation, Foley disclosed that he was gay, an alcoholic, and had been molested by a clergyman as a child. He immediately checked himself into alcohol rehabilitation as his Republican colleagues attempted to distance themselves from him.

The Foley story was disturbing and ironic on a number of levels. Many felt it was illustrative of the party's hypocrisy. At least the Republicans' opponents wanted to expand it to such a level. They may not have been totally wrong. During the summer of 2005, Foley introduced legislation to shield children from adult exploitation over the Internet. Not only did he push the legislation hard, but he was, in fact, the chairman of the House Missing and Exploited Children's Caucus. This quagmire got deeper when the *Washington Post* reported that some in GOP leadership knew about Foley's habit as early as 2000—long before it was made public.[12] The ripple ran all the way to the top with calls from some quarters for the resignation of Speaker of the House Dennis Hastert.

What's Wrong with the Democrats?

The Republicans' implosion did little for the Democrats other than make it clear that the Democrats were so woeful they could not "win" anything. The Republicans had to "lose." As the 2006 elections approached to set up the presidential showdown in 2008, the GOP's mounting list of inconsistencies, questionable domestic policy decisions, global missteps, and outright scandals finally took their toll. In effect, the Democrats benefited mightily from Republican failures rather than their own successes. Because of the emptied-out talent level of his party, Barack Obama was now actually receiving pressure from many quarters to run for president. While he and those close to him continued to deny any interest in throwing his hat into the presidential ring, Obama's actions sometimes betrayed his comments. In September 2006, he was the special guest of Iowa Senator Tom Harkin at his annual steak fry at the Warren County Fairgrounds in Indianola, Iowa. Harkin had hosted the event for the past twenty-nine years, and it had become a regular stop for Democratic presidential hopefuls. Of course, Obama explained his presence away by saying he was only there to help fellow Democrats in the midterm elections, not to pursue his own political ambitions. Many observers had legitimate doubts.

Despite the reservations of a few, most people across lines of race *and* political party loved Obama. In the 2004 Illinois race, he won a stunning 40 percent of the state's Republican vote. Even this, upon closer examination, was largely the result of more strange Republican behavior. In June 2004, just prior to the November elections, Republican nominee Jack Ryan dropped out of the race. He did so after child custody hearing testimony was made public in which his exwife (actress Jeri Ryan) accused him of insisting she go to "explicit sex clubs" in New York, New Orleans, and Paris during their marriage—including a bizarre club with cages, whips, and other apparatuses hanging from the ceiling. She testified that Ryan also wanted her to have sex with him while others watched. Ryan dismissed his exwife's allegations as "ridiculous accusations" but eventually yielded under the pressure and left the race.[13]

The Republicans' last minute replacement in a hopeless race? Conservative Alan Keyes freshly transplanted from Maryland. Even before Ryan's implosion, he was polling a bit behind Obama. After his exit, the cause was lost. Even serious conservative politicos considered Keyes little more than a political dilettante who posed no real challenge. Hence, Obama's immediate political future was sealed. Upon observation, it is easy to see that "Obamamania" was more a result of a series of unfortunate (and unsavory) events than individual achievements. In many respects, Obama is the product of timing. The political bar was lowered so horribly by missteps by both parties that Obama did not have to do much beyond deliver a cliché-filled, nonoffensive speech to endear himself to many disgruntled and desperate Americans.

Does being the beneficiary of advantageous timing make Barack Obama a bad person, yet undiscovered seedy politician, or untrustworthy leader? Absolutely not. On the flip side of that coin, these factors do not necessarily make him great either. So, what is wrong with him? Frankly, in the political reality in which we live and languish, very little. But, from a progressive's point of view, nothing is terribly right with him either. To be sure, he is all the things mentioned above and more. Doubters (and worriers) believe the greatest source of his appeal is also his greatest problem: he seems painfully "safe." He presents no discernible threat to the status quo.

The first red flag for some was actually raised a few days after the nation began to hear of Obama outside of Illinois. During the 2004 Democratic National Convention and before his now classic speech, when asked by a reporter about the Democrats' concern that all speakers toe the party line, Obama replied that he had no problem staying on message. In fact, Tavis Smiley seemed to confirm Obama's flexibility when he reported the next week that Obama allowed personally important parts of his speech that Democratic presidential nominee John Kerry's campaign team found disagreeable to be "excised." Yet, during his oration before the Democratic Convention and the nation (with no mention of the censorship by his own party) Obama still referred to America as a "magical place."[14] Unfortunately, neither Obama's nor the Democrats' "message" was convincing enough as the Democrats (not including Obama) were once again drubbed on election day.

Immediately after the election, Princeton public intellectual Cornel West commented that 70 percent of the people who voted for President Bush believed there was a direct link between al-Qaeda and Saddam Hussein. One in three still believed Iraq had weapons of mass destruction (WMD). Research by the nonpartisan Program on International Policy Attitudes (PIPA) echoed West's sentiment. An October 2004 PIPA survey of Bush supporters just prior to the election concluded that 72 percent believed Iraq either had WMD or a major WMD program just before the war. Even after chief U.S. weapons inspector Charles Duelfer reported to the contrary, 56 percent of Bush supporters mistakenly believed most experts said Iraq had WMD. The same percentage also believed Iraq was either directly involved in September 11 or provided al-Qaeda substantial support.[15]

Interestingly, when drawing a link between information sources and perceptions of reality, PIPA concluded that people who predominantly got their news from National Public Radio (NPR) or Public Broadcasting Service (PBS) held beliefs on world realities that were closest to the truth. Those who primarily got their info from Fox News had views that were farthest from the truth. Most Bush supporters reported that Fox News was their primary news source. To be sure, some of our national troubles are fueled by the media, but as West said, much of it is also indicative of "deliberate ignorance and willful blindness on behalf of many fellow citizens."[16] Without a doubt, a good percentage of our citizenry is in denial or so wrapped up in its own international and domestic neonationalistic mean-spiritedness that the country has been placed on a path many consider retrograde.

This environment of myopia, narrow religious and political dogma, and narcissistic self-absorption enabled Bush political strategist Karl Rove to author a plan he felt would mobilize more than 4 million Evangelical Christians to support Bush prior to the 2004 presidential election.

Even in the face of inner circle concerns that Rove's plan lurched the Bush camp too far to the right, Rove successfully blurred the line between church and state and exceeded his goal by actually motivating more than 8 million Christian fundamentalists to pull the lever for Bush in his successful reelection bid. By strategically injecting gay marriage and abortion into the fray, the Rove Plan carved out space for the paternalistic, homophobic, religiously intolerant Christian Right to take center stage in American politics and public policy.

Christian fundamentalists effectively cloaked intolerance in the guise of "morality," wrapping themselves in the American flag and beating their opponents' challenges back with the Bible. Not surprisingly, a certain percentage of socially conservative, religiously devout blacks all too willingly joined these ranks. In 2004, black electoral support for Bush actually rose roughly 3 percent from 2000 rather than declined.[17] Meanwhile, the Democrats sat silently and accepted their fate. Their "message" was unclear. Their candidates, headed by the doomed John Kerry, were largely uninspiring. Their strategies seemed reactionary instead of proactive and progressive. And their imagination had seemingly left the building with Bill Clinton four years earlier.

In the minds of some, the most serious problem with Obama's commitment to staying on the empty Democratic "message" was not simply that the party's message lacked clarity and conviction. The greatest difficulty was more troubling. When he proclaimed he had no problem staying on message, he seemed to forget (or maybe he never knew) that those who have really impacted the world—the true visionaries—have frequently stayed *off message*. There are a few other potential problems with Obama that merit consideration. Some argue that he shares one with another Democratic celebrity and 2008 presidential opponent: Hillary Clinton. For all his faults, Bill Clinton actually seemed to believe in something. However, many see his wife as a purely political animal guided by, more than anything, the pursuit of power, often seeming willing to say and do whatever to garner and maintain it. She plays the American political power game well and usually stays "on message."

Others believe Obama shares another problem with America. In our current political haze, we have forgotten that there is not only a gap between political reality and political imagination, but a yawning chasm. Jeffrey H. Reiman articulates it well in his book *In Defense of Political Philosophy*:

> The politics of a nation is one thing; its political imagination is quite another. Politics amounts to the day-to-day decisions and actions of

politicians and their audiences. But political imagination refers to that sense of connection between the real and the ideal, and the boundary between the possible and the utopian, which is felt before it is reasoned out.[18]

Undoubtedly, Barack Obama is great at slotting himself into the existing political reality. Unfortunately, though many horribly unimaginative Americans see Obama as ingenious (everything is relative), he may have, in actuality, sacrificed his political imagination somewhere along the way. This is the site where we locate his greatest danger. He presents an image that exudes and engenders hope. He even made it the centerpiece of his latest book, *The Audacity of Hope*. But is he capable of delivering? He offers light-hearted, nonconfrontational rhetoric about change, but no clear vision or discernible commitment to it where certain issues are concerned. Unlike Corey Booker, Michael Steele, Kenneth Blackwell, and others, we do not know exactly who and what Barack Obama is. Many, however, see Obama as a political savior and have, therefore, invested all their hopes, dreams, and imaginative energy in him. Unfortunately, he may not have as much of these as his supporters. They are committed to the belief that Obama is "different." But is he?

Et Tu, Obama?

When faced with the question of whether or not Obama is committed to a progressive vision, the most commonly encountered argument is that this once again simply raises the age-old debate between working within the system or "crashing" it. At the presidential level of politics, is that even a choice? Americans with living political imaginations not only answer, "Yes, we have a choice," but take it a step farther and proclaim, "We also have a duty!" Political party, racial, and ideological differences aside, let us, for a moment, think as responsible Americans of good conscience who live in the most powerful country in the world. Republican losses in 2006 confirmed that a revisit of America's approach to the world is in order. In the post–September 11 world, any analysis must begin with the United States' sojourn into Iraq and its implications on the global stage. From the outset, the mission to "free Iraq" became so clouded by emotion and chest thumping that it was difficult to have a balanced discussion if one did not wholeheartedly buy into the mainstream Bush administration party line.

Considering the fact the United States now flexes a level of military muscle relative to the rest of the world not seen since the apex of the Roman Empire, there was little doubt that Iraq's military would be quickly defeated. Post-Saddam, nontraditional resistance and consequences, of course, are other matters altogether. Beyond military might, America has become the modern Rome in other troubling ways. In *The Twilight of American Culture* (2000), Morris Berman notes that America resembles Rome immediately preceding its decline in four key ways. Both experienced the following: (1) accelerating social and economic inequality; (2) declining marginal returns with regard to investment in organizational solutions to socioeconomic problems; (3) rapidly dropping levels of literacy, critical understanding, and general intellectual awareness; and (4) spiritual death or the emptying out of cultural content and the freezing of it in formulas (clichés, media slogans, sound bites, etc.).

In one of his most powerful passages, Berman says that once a nation reaches this point,

> In the classicist phrase, the culture no longer believes in itself, so it typically undertakes phony or misguided wars (Vietnam, or Gulf War I, for example), or promotes its symbols and slogans all the more. As the organizational costs rise, yielding increasingly smaller benefits, so does the formalism, the pomp and circumstance. Just as the jaded crowds of ancient Rome zoned out on bread and circuses, Hollywood makes Rocky-type films, rerunning tired old formulas, but nevertheless, these are box office hits. And gladiatorial extravaganzas, as well as the "Rambification" of culture, are sure signs of spiritual death.[19]

The great question ignored in the midst of American self-congratulation and hubris is, How will the rest of the world approach the twenty-first century's Rome? Americans may lament how a good portion of the world hates their way of life and freedom, but another possibility is that many now sincerely fear what they see as American aggression. The United States has been able to maintain its position as the world's only super power without serious challenge for quite some time. The reasons behind this reality are multivariate, but one of the most important has been the fact that a decent percentage of the world has generally viewed America as benevolent.

Flying in the face of world opinion, at the turn of the century many felt the country displayed a disturbing propensity for overt callousness, unilateral decision making and bullying. The feeling that "America does what America wants" and, in the words of George W. Bush, "If you're not with us, you're against us," has left many of Earth's inhabitants asking, "Whom will America go after next?" So, one issue beyond Iraq is apparent. When one country rises to a level of power and influence clearly disproportionate to its neighbors and is perceived as abusing that power, the neighbors are forced to engage in "balancing behavior." That is, many countries that would otherwise have nothing in common may come together to establish a political and military "balance" to keep America, the new Rome, at bay. This perception certainly prompted Russian president and 2007 *Time* Person of the Year Vladimir Putin to rail against the United States at the Munich Conference on Security Policy, an annual forum attracting senior officials from around the world, in February 2007. Putin blamed U.S. policy for inciting other countries to seek nuclear weapons to defend themselves from an "almost uncontained use of military force." He went on:

> Unilateral, illegitimate actions have not solved a single problem, they have become a hotbed of further conflicts. . . . One state, the United States, has overstepped its national borders in every way. . . . It is a world of one master, one sovereign. . . . It has nothing to do with democracy. This is nourishing the wish of countries to get nuclear weapons. . . . This is very dangerous. Nobody feels secure anymore because nobody can hide behind international law. . . . The process of NATO expansion has nothing to do with modernization of the alliance or with ensuring security in Europe. On the contrary, it is a serious factor provoking reduction of mutual trust.[20]

U.S. Senator John McCain, (R-Arizona) described Putin's remarks as "the most aggressive speech from a Russian leader since the end of the Cold War."[21] No matter how distasteful to American leadership, the international possibilities raised by Putin warrant consideration. Meanwhile, trouble also looms domestically. Continued poverty, a staggering national debt, festering racism, classism, religious intolerance, homophobia, corporate malfeasance, and other factors have created an untenable situation for many Americans.

These factors considered, the individual case of Barack Obama is only an example that speaks to a much larger problem. He is not the sickness. He is simply the latest and most popular symptom. Interrogating our approaches to the Obamas of the world tells us much more than examining these individuals ever could. We are now a pessimistic nation with little belief in the possibility for change and decency—

especially through politics. This hopelessness, this perception that we have no personal or collective efficacy, has led us to a place where we not only accept mediocrity—we celebrate it. We do not condemn debauchery; we ignore it. The effects are Novocainlike in that we have all been anesthetized to some degree.

In this quagmire, was anyone really shocked by the Mark Foley revelations? Was anyone surprised that there exists not the possibility but the probability that leading members of our government attempted to cover it up? Has anyone really been disturbed by the ever-increasing list of our leaders caught up in the Jack Abramoff scandal? How many have been genuinely angered by Randy "Duke" Cunningham, William Jefferson, or Bob Ney? Does anyone believe Alberto Gonzalez, Karl Rove, or "Scooter" Libby? Does anyone think Dick Cheney was not involved in Libby's actions? Did the president not know? Did he really commute Libby's sentence just because he felt it was "excessive," or was this yet another display of the administration's gangsterism? How many care that the Bush administration may have lied to involve the country in Iraq? Who cares that the Democrats were complicitous (even though they would like us to forget that now)? Did people not note the contradiction when the president stood on an aircraft carrier and declared, "Mission accomplished," but kept sending fathers, mothers, brothers, sisters, sons, daughters, and friends off to die? Do citizens really believe that every leader who disagrees with our government is a tyrant or madman? Do they care that politicians, no matter their party, flip-flop more than fish out of water? Do Americans really trust politicians anymore— any of them? When was the last time you actually voted *for* a candidate rather than *against* one?

Is this what we have become? Deceived and numb? Hopeless and oblivious? Those who maintain political imaginations are not seeking the impossible. In fact, they are our last hope. They are merely asking for leaders who stand for something, not politicians who insult us with safe positions and empty clichés. They want leaders who tell the truth—be it good or bad. That is not crashing the system. That is making it work properly. Is Obama, the self-proclaimed "skinny guy with the funny name," the answer? Many would certainly say, "Yes," but for different reasons. Their reasons are often different because, as Cal Thomas observed immediately after Obama formed an exploratory committee to decide whether to run for president in January 2007, "Part of the attraction and seductiveness of Senator Obama—perhaps the main attraction—is that he is mostly a blank slate on which others can write what they choose." He closed his article, "[There are] questions that need answering. We have a right to know what manner of individual aspires to the Oval Office, before we give him, or her, the honor, privilege and responsibility of the office. In short, it's time to start writing on that blank slate and to seriously contemplate what's written there."[22]

Agree with Thomas or not, his stance warrants reflection. Despite the enthusiasm associated with Obamamania, people knew very little about where he stood on most serious issues when his presidential aspirations were finally made apparent in early 2007. Without a doubt, he intentionally sought to maintain the "blank canvas, be all things to all people" image as long as he could. Nevertheless, as the searing lights of a presidential candidacy heated, he would soon be more exposed than ever. In "New Rome," would Obama be remembered for the selfless commitment of Marcus Aurelius or the treachery of Marcus Brutus? By now, he was considered not only a black leader but also a part of American leadership. In many minds, he was also the leader with the greatest potential to change the world—a daunting expectation indeed.

Even among the riders of the Obamamania wave, some seemed somewhat concerned by Obama's sometimes pliable approach and political amiability. Cornel West has commented that Obama seems to see himself as a "voluntary immigrant" and consequently lacks the "rage" connected to those who see themselves as the descendants of "involuntary immigrants."[23] Despite the observation, West does not dismiss Obama's possibilities:

> It's very difficult for people with a blemished record to run for office. And it's hard for people to have an unblemished record. We all are tainted. We all are cracked vessels. We all are imperfect. If you're looking for purity, you have to look hard because we're all impure. People who claim to be pure are just lying and hiding something. But I have great hope for Brother Obama.[24]

To be sure, Obama needs West's hope and prayers. The entire country does.

2

Sorry, Du Bois Doesn't Live Here Anymore

The Soulessness of the New Talented Tenth

Without education, there is no hope for our people; and without hope, our future is lost.
—Charles Hamilton Houston (popular quote, unsourced)

To increase abiding satisfaction for the mass of our people, and for all people, someone must sacrifice something of his own happiness. This is a duty only to those who recognize it as a duty. It is silly to tell intelligent human beings: Be good and you will be happy. The truth is today, be good, be decent, be honorable and self-sacrificing and you will not always be happy. You will often be desperately unhappy. You may even be crucified, dead, and buried, and the third day you will be just as dead as the first. But with the death of your happiness may easily come the increased happiness and satisfaction and fulfillment for other people—strangers, unborn babes, uncreated worlds. If this is not sufficient incentive, never try it—remain hogs!
—W. E. B. Du Bois, Howard University Commencement Address, Washington, D.C. (1930)

Though often overlooked, 1895 was one of the most important years in the evolution of black leadership in America. In February 1895, Frederick Douglass, the exslave and undisputed greatest black leader of the nineteenth century who fought most of his life to force

America to live up to its ideals, died. The "Lion of Anacostia" was many things—self-educated, escaped slave, author, newspaper publisher, orator, abolitionist, and thief. Thief? Ah, yes—the most noble sort. Douglass often labeled himself as such proclaiming to audiences on the abolitionist lecture circuit of the mid-1800s, "I appear before you this evening as a thief and a robber. I stole this head, these limbs, this body from my master and ran off with them." Indeed! Douglass provided a standard to which most black leadership after him could only aspire. His death left a yawning void in leadership for a people experiencing one of its nadir periods in post-Reconstruction America.

Less than seven months after Douglass passed, Charles Hamilton Houston was born in September 1895. After finishing his undergraduate work at Amherst and a stint in the army, Houston entered Harvard Law School in 1919. His exceptional grades eventually enabled him to become the first black to serve on the prestigious *Harvard Law Review* editorial board. Houston graduated in the top 5 percent of his class and went on to work on the Doctor of Juridical Science degree. During this time, Houston decided Jim Crow segregation, legally established as a result of the *Plessy v. Ferguson* decision of 1896, must also be eradicated using the law. In 1924, after traveling in Algeria, Spain, and Tunisia, Houston returned to America to begin his assault. Douglass O. Linder writes:

> For Charles Houston, the training of black lawyers was a key to mounting a successful attack on segregation. While at Harvard, Houston wrote that "there must be Negro lawyers in every community" and that "the great majority" of these lawyers "must come from Negro schools." It was, he concluded, "in the best interests of the United States . . . to provide the best teachers possible" at law schools where Negroes might be trained. Houston decided to seek a teaching position at Howard Law School, which since its establishment in 1869 had trained three-fourths of the black lawyers in the United States. He enlisted notable members of the Harvard faculty, including Dean Roscoe Pound and future Supreme Court Justice Felix Frankfurter to write letters in support of his application. Pound's letter assured Howard that Houston "gives promise of becoming a real legal scholar." In the fall of 1924, Professor Charles Houston began teaching "Agency," "Surety and Mortgages," "Jurisprudence," and "Administrative Law" to first- and second-year law students at Howard.[1]

Less than five years later, Houston would not only become a "real legal scholar" but Howard Law School's vice-dean. By then he was firmly on a course to train an impressive cadre of young black lawyers to fight for what he called "the social good." Over time, some of these young people would join Houston in forming the core of the now legendary NAACP legal defense team that eventually overturned *Plessy* with the 1954 *Brown v. Board* decision. Among them was Thurgood Marshall. Though Houston died in 1950 before *Brown* was argued, he, not Marshall, is really the "man who killed Jim Crow." Speaking of Houston, Marshall reverently claimed, "We were just carrying his bags—that's all."[2]

Black America endured almost fifty years of legal segregation (and more de facto years after that) before the victory of Houston's legal team in 1954. Disturbing to some, segregation was never strongly challenged by Frederick Douglass' immediate "successor" as premier black American leader. Before Houston could speak, the man who would become the most powerful black of the early twentieth century would take the national stage in 1895. On September 18, fifteen days after Houston's birth, Booker Taliaferro Washington delivered his infamous (to some) "Atlanta Exposition Address" to an all white audience in Atlanta's Piedmont Park. Washington set forth a paradigm that would all but guarantee he would replace Douglass as black America's newest and most influential power broker until his death twenty years later. The following famous passage from the speech exemplify Washington's "accomodationist" politics:

> Casting down your bucket among my people, helping and encouraging them as you are doing on these grounds, and to education of head, hand, and heart, you will find that they will buy your surplus land, make blossom the waste places in your fields, and run your factories. While doing this, you can be sure in the future, as in the past, that you and your families will be surrounded by the most patient, faithful, law-abiding, and unresentful people that the world has seen. As we have proved our loyalty to you in the past, nursing your children, watching by the sick-bed of your mothers and fathers, and often following them with tear-dimmed eyes to their graves, so in the future, in our humble way, we shall stand by you with a devotion that no foreigner can approach, ready to lay down our lives, if need be, in defense of yours, interlacing our industrial, commercial, civil, and religious life with yours in a way that shall make the interests of both races one. In all things that are purely social we can be as separate as the fingers, yet one as the hand in all things essential to mutual progress.[3]

Of course, Washington was not alone on the black leadership land-scape as America entered the twentieth century. Also in 1895, William Edward Burghardt Du Bois completed his graduate studies at Harvard. Like Houston (with whom Du Bois crossed paths later in life) serving on the *Harvard Law Review* editorial board, Du Bois's graduation was groundbreaking: he was the first black to earn a Ph.D. from the presti-gious university. Du Bois would go on to become one of America's most influential intellectuals and famously proclaimed that the major prob-lem of the twentieth century would be the "problem of the color-line." He was only partially right. It seems that not only was the color line the major problem of the 20th century, but it is shaping up to be one of the most corrosive irritants of the twenty-first century as well. Throughout his ninety-five years of life, Du Bois unfailingly believed education was an essential tool in solving it.

Across leadership communities, from religion to politics to media and entertainment; from Du Bois to Houston to Jesse Jackson to Barack Obama, most modern black leaders usually have at least one thing in common: they are educated and, therefore, members of what Du Bois labeled the "Talented Tenth." Du Bois presented a number of perspec-tives on this group of black educated elites. They were the source of both great hope and deep-seated frustration for him. Even today, opin-ions on the Talented Tenth's place in the black freedom struggle vary, but few evaluators of the subject disagree that education plays an important role in the shaping of minds and their approaches to racial uplift. Therefore, a continuous reevaluation of the dominant educa-tional paradigm in use at American postsecondary institutions, which Brazilian educator Paulo Freire called the "banking education" model, must be at the heart of our concerns when we consider the sociopoliti-cal orientation of the Talented Tenth of the twenty-first century.

Freire opines that the banking model is an institutional tool that, intentionally or unintentionally, hampers emancipatory thought among disenfranchised groups because of its purely narrational charac-ter. While some form of narration is usually present in identity forma-tion, in many cases this narration may be oppressive instead of genera-tive. Freire believed the banking model uses narration as a socializing agent that does not engender but combats critical consciousness:[4]

Narration (with the teacher as narrator) leads the students to mem-orize mechanically the narrated content. . . . Education thus becomes an act of depositing, in which the students are the depositories and the teacher is the depositor. Instead of communicating, the teacher issues communiques and makes deposits which the students patiently receive, memorize, and repeat. . . . It is not surprising that the banking concept of education regards men as adaptable, manageable beings. The more students work at storing the deposits entrusted to them, the less they develop the critical consciousness which would result in their intervention in the world as transformers of the world.[5]

Through such a process, "the scope of action allowed to the students extends only as far as receiving, filing, and storing the deposits."[6] The key concern with the banking model is that stances on what is legitimate or emancipatory knowledge are largely subjective. Through decisions on which knowledge is acceptable, desirable, and respected, teachers (as the guardians and pawns) of educational structures regulate how the world enters into students as well as how students enter into the world. Logically, dominant group educational structures are not overly concerned with empowering the dominated. Consequently, in our examination of current realities influencing the formation of the modern black vanguard, the generative and degenerative results of the banking model need scrutiny. Ultimately, our endeavor is to use the banking model as the nexus from which to couple the historical evolution of Du Bois's concept of the Talented Tenth with Freire's idea of liberatory education that encourages learners to challenge and change the world, not merely adapt to it.

Revisiting Du Bois's Talented Tenth

Contrary to popular belief, W. E. B. Du Bois did not coin the phrase *Talented Tenth*, but he popularized it in his essay of the same name that first appeared in a volume edited, ironically, by Booker T. Washington entitled *The Negro Problem* in 1903.[7] In this essay Du Bois theorized, "The Negro race, like all races, is going to be saved by its exceptional men."[8] He strongly believed these "exceptional men" would necessarily rise from the ranks of the educated, and their duty was to bring out the best in the race by guiding the "Mass [of Negroes] away from the contamination and death of the Worst, in their own and other races."[9] Du Bois contended that education was essential in producing not only educated people but also ones with a clear mission concerning the race. He commented:

> Now the training of men is a difficult task. Its technique is a matter for educational experts, but its object is for the vision of seers. If we

make money the object of man-training, we shall develop money-makers but not necessarily men; if we make technical skill the object of education, we may possess artisans but not, in nature, men. Men we shall have only as we make manhood the object of the work of schools—intelligence, broad sympathy, knowledge of the world that was and is, and of the relation of men to it—this is the curriculum of Higher Education which must underlie true life.[10]

It is important to note that Du Bois was not simply speaking of the ascent to adulthood when he spoke of making "manhood the object of the work of schools." Contrarily, the point of his argument is that the main goal of education should be the cultivation of sociopolitical maturity in students so that they would be better able to aid in the forward movement of black people. The mission of higher education, therefore, was to produce a cadre of black activist intellectuals whose primary goal was the creation of an egalitarian society. An essential step in creating such a world would be the destruction of the perception of blacks as either subhuman or superhuman (depending on the circumstances), but simply human. Theoretically, the realization of such humanization should ultimately shift the foci of most questions concerning race and other associated cleavages to broader, collective human concerns. No individual effort (educational, economic, psychological, social, political, etc.) is singularly more important than others in this humanization project, but collectively all of them contribute to the noble and needed objective of human liberation.

For Du Bois, the impact of the Talented Tenth on the black humanization project would be essential and necessarily twofold: internal to and external to the race. Internal to the race, the Talented Tenth would present hope and guidance for the supposedly directionless masses. Evaluations of the Talented Tenth doctrine in its original form that characterize it as elitist are indisputable. There is no avoiding this fact when Du Bois's own words are recalled: "Can the masses of the Negro people be in any possible way more quickly raised than by the effort and example of this aristocracy of talent and character? Was there ever a nation on God's fair earth civilized from the bottom upward? Never; it is, ever was and ever will be from the top downward that culture filters."[11] Despite the clear highbrow nature of this passage, history supports Du Bois's stance that liberatory thought flowing from the top downward rather than vice-versa is more realistic than the contention that a collective psychological revolution among the oppressed masses will somehow autonomously manifest itself.[12]

For those who do not regard elites as naturally villainous, the idea of the Talented Tenth is not inherently destructive. Antithetically, it may very well be mandatory for group progress. Approaches that place ultimate faith in the appearance of a collective revolutionary consciousness have not proven realistic or reliable. The histories of most societies illustrate that massification produces people who are just as (or even more) prone to become delinquents, cynics, or nihilists as they are to become revolutionary thinkers and agents. Praxis, therefore, is not spontaneous, but is born of intellectual observation and understanding of the complexities involved in sociopolitical marginalization and subsequent planning and action to overcome it. Unfortunate for critics who demonize Talented Tenth theory, such engagement and action are usually not brought to fruition by undirected masses.

In addition to its internal effect on blacks, external to the race the Talented Tenth would also serve to convince nonblacks that blacks were indeed capable of noble and civilized achievement:

> Do Americans ever stop to reflect that there are in this land a million men of Negro blood, well-educated, owners of homes, against the honor of whose womanhood no breath was ever raised, whose men occupy positions of trust and usefulness, and who, judged by any standard, *have reached the full measure of the best type of modern European culture?* (emphasis added).[13]

An obvious problem for Du Bois at this point was the fact that he engaged in cultural mislocation by centering on Europe.[14] This is the same predicament cogently addressed by Harold Cruse in *The Crisis of the Negro Intellectual* and echoed by others. Cruse and others have contended blacks face both economic and political crises. They also contend that the crisis of culture is critical. While Du Bois showed flashes of coming to grips with this realization in *Dusk of Dawn*, he ultimately fell short. He was not alone in this failure and it has resulted in historical, as well as contemporary, attempts by black elites to reach "the full measure of the best type of modern European culture." The problem with such a striving is that, for the most part, European culture has neither spoken to nor respected the African descended experience. If the Talented Tenth views such an achievement as a goal without the promotion of generative black cultural norms and mores, the "example of this aristocracy" and the culture that "filters" to the masses stands a great chance of being decentered and destructive. Consequently, even though Du Bois began to realize that his original conceptualization of the Talented Tenth was flawed, he failed to understand that one of his major errors was not his faith in black elites, but his embracing of European culture and its perspectives on what was desirable, good, and successful.

Joy James' *Transcending the Talented Tenth* is an important study because it calls latter twentieth-century interpretations of Du Bois's Talented Tenth into question. James submits that commentaries on the Talented Tenth that do not take Du Bois's later evaluations of the concept into account are shortsighted and not truly Du Boisian. This is so, according to James, because the older, "Marxist" Du Bois rejected much of what he asserted at the turn of the century concerning an educated black elite trained to lead the race in social, political, and cultural struggle. She criticizes diverse groups and individuals ranging from the Black Panthers to Cornel West and Henry Louis Gates as black elites who, in one way or another, fail or refuse to recognize and acknowledge Du Bois's shift. James feels such ideologies are the result of selfish "vanguard elitism." She believes this elitism is central to the hampering of any effort to truly democratize intellectual ability and herald the coming of a viable sense of agency among the masses in the black community.

James notes that Talented Tenth theory in its original form was unquestionably elitist, but she believes Du Bois began to "inch toward democratic reform" and away from this black elitism in his autobiography *Dusk of Dawn*. She acquiesces, however, that even as he made this shift, he continued to identify "black elites as natural leadership."[15] James then argues that Du Bois later deconstructed the Talented Tenth in his 1948 speech, "The Talented Tenth: Memorial Address." It could also be argued, however, that Du Bois did not bury Talented Tenth theory, but resurrected and reinforced it by laying out an agenda for a group of black elites he dubbed the "Guiding Hundredth."[16] This progression of reducing the "Tenth" to a "Hundredth" makes perfect sense when we realize that Du Bois made these modifications as he spoke to his fraternity brothers of Sigma Pi Phi (also known as the Boule), an organization so elitist that Du Bois's simple membership in it serves as a testament to his continued bourgeois inclinations. Paradoxically, such was the company Du Bois kept: an organization of men that celebrated materialism and elitism, even though many contend that by this time he had become a Marxist.

Whether or not Du Bois continued to champion the idea of the Talented Tenth, we must face a disturbing reality concerning blacks and postsecondary education that continues to this day. If we concede (as Du Bois did) that college-educated blacks are the true members of this vanguard group, then they continue to make up little more than a tenth of black America's population. James notes that no generation of blacks in America has graduated more than 15 percent from college. Even if one does not adhere to the notion of the Talented Tenth, this is an important statistic, because research has consistently yielded strong correlations between education and financial and sociopolitical advancement for individuals as well as groups. Be it a positive or negative reality of our society, college education has a definite impact on the life chances of most American citizens. An argument can certainly be made that Du Bois recognized a serious error in his original framework without totally abandoning the notion of the necessity of black elite leadership. He commented in *Dusk of Dawn*, "The power of this aristocracy of talent was to lie in its knowledge and character and not in its wealth. The problem which I did not then attack was that of leadership and authority within the group, which by implication left controls to wealth—a contingency of which I never dreamed."[17]

It becomes clear from the above passage that another of Du Bois's major initial mistakes was his failure to consider inescapable American socialization and its impact on the Talented Tenth. Of course, he eventually realized that without counters to the individualism that permeates American society, the Talented Tenth would necessarily be ineffective and misguided for it would be plagued with the selfishness and folly of materialism. The checks to these ills for the young Du Bois were the professors he encountered at Fisk University. By his own admission, his New England rearing gave him no real sense of responsibility to the race. Fisk centered him:

> I assumed that with knowledge, sacrifice would automatically follow. In my youth and idealism, I did not realize that selfishness is even more natural than sacrifice. I made the assumption of its wide availability because of the spirit of sacrifice learned in my mission school training. . . . At Fisk I met a group of teachers who would be unusual in any time or place. They were not only men of learning and experience, but men and women of character and almost fanatic devotion. It was a great experience to sit under their voice and influence. It was from that experience that I assumed easily that educated people, in most cases were going out into life to see how far they could better the world.[18]

Unfortunately, Du Bois's assumption was wrong, and it became painfully clear to him that all Fisk students were not of the sacrificing sort. To the contrary, many were quite selfish. He notes:

There was no lack of small and selfish souls; there were among the student body, careless and lazy fellows; and there were especially sharp young persons, who received the education given very cheaply at Fisk University, with the distinct and single-minded idea, of seeing how much they could make out of it for themselves, and nobody else.[19]

Critical Consciousness and the Humanization Project

Regardless of the criticisms of his theoretical and personal shortcomings, few would disagree with Du Bois's assertion that the Talented Tenth should ultimately be concerned with bettering the world. However, the pressing issue at this juncture is what types of educational strategies help develop such a commitment in students who are immersed in a society that champions compartmentalized social and political structures. It is here the deployment of Freire and his idea of critical consciousness can aid us in constructing practical responses to educational models that do not encourage the Talented Tenth to dedicate itself to the collective transformation of the world beyond spheres of individualism. Du Bois's reference to the responsibility to "see how far [one] could better the world" engendered at Fisk was an illustration of what some social critics (academic or lay) would label "consciousness."

It would certainly be easy for us to (and many do) assume that the Fisk students who followed the path of service to the race were conscious, and those whom Du Bois called "small and selfish souls" were not. To be fair, however, beyond this personal moral judgment a clear definition of a conscious Talented Tenth can be difficult to ascertain. Perspectives on consciousness range from the activist stance that it signifies a person's recognition of (and dedication to remedying) sociopolitical strife to the academic supposition that it can simply be defined as rational-critical thought. Whatever definition one accepts, however, consciousness loses much of its importance outside of the realm of rhetoric in the black freedom struggle if its goal is not to supply the marginalized black collective with some modicum of agency and humanity. If consciousness is indeed emptied of its relevance when it does not seek to alter oppressive structures, then we may be faced not only with normative philosophical issues but with praxis concerns as well.

Despite the often-encountered debates as to what constitutes true consciousness, Freire was clear as to what he thought consciousness was and how it should be used once gained. Freire's best-known work, *Pedagogy of the Oppressed*, engaged the dilemmas of oppressed people in his homeland of Brazil, which has historically been plagued by issues of class and color discrimination. While *Pedagogy* was not originally written to analyze the conditions of African Americans, it is certainly relevant to the struggles of this population. One of the central variables at the heart of *Pedagogy* as well as other works by Freire was the idea of consciousness that he saw as essential for liberatory teaching. It must be understood that Freire strongly believed *conscientizacao* (conscientization) was a necessary but not sufficient condition for positive social change (positive change being the eventual humanization of the world by the oppressed).[20] Freire regarded the humanization project as a life vocation in contrast to the historical aberration of dehumanization heaped upon peripheralized peoples by the oppressor. Dehumanization, which Freire believed to be reinforced by the banking model of education, is characterized by cynicism among the oppressed at best and by their total despair at worst.

Beyond this, the reality of dehumanization often causes the oppressor to heap violence upon the oppressed as he attempts to maintain his station in society. Maybe even more disturbing, the sociopolitical conditions brought on by dehumanization promote nihilism and intragroup violence as a result of psychic trauma among the oppressed. Freire felt that, ultimately, it must be the oppressed who bring the humanization project into existence, because the oppressor will not voluntarily surrender his position of dominance. Like Marx's engagement of the revolt of the proletariat, Freire makes it clear that the goal of the oppressed must not be to become oppressors of the former oppressor but to restore the humanity of both groups.

Sitting at the core of Freire's contribution to the humanization project is the mandate that the oppressed can only move forward after achieving critical consciousness. According to Freire, critical consciousness consisted of three interrelated stages: semi-intransitivity, naive transitivity, and critical transitivity. The first stage, "semi-intransitive consciousness," is consciousness that is uncritical, inactive, and does not challenge the world.[21] Tom Heancy summarizes semi-intransitive consciousness as "the state of those whose sphere of perception is limited, whose interests center almost totally around matters of survival, and who are impermeable to challenges situated outside the demands of biological necessity."[22]

The reasons for semi-intransitivity are numerous. It may be a product of dogmatic interpersonal socialization that teaches one not to question institutional authority and structures. It may also be a matter of necessity for those who exist on the peasant level of society.

Unfortunately, it is usually unrealistic to expect those who suffer from abject poverty to construct new paradigms for liberating the world instead of securing means to feed themselves and their children from day to day. For this growing population, simple physical survival is a daily struggle that does not allow ample opportunity for engagement and resolution of the structural problems of American society. Unfortunately, while semi-intransitivity is understandable, it does not contribute to the humanization project.

Many who are never forced to confront daily survival issues and/or those who overcome them may move to the second stage of consciousness: "naive transitivity." This stage is often encountered among young would-be radicals who purport that the remedies to black suffering are to be found in a glorious past of activism. It is here we locate those who fancy themselves keepers of the faith by reciting quotes from Malcolm, Martin, or Marcus. Ironically, it is also here that we locate intolerant conservatives who believe America is suffering because of a loss of generally accepted "glory days" values from the 1950s and early 1960s. Those at the naive transitive stage often have minimal understanding of the real issues that confront contemporary America and only a dash of substance behind their charismatic style:

> Freire characterizes this stage of consciousness by an over-simplification of problems, nostalgia for the past, an underestimation of ordinary people, a strong tendency to gregariousness, a disinterest in investigation, a fascination with fanciful explanations of reality, and by the practice of polemics rather than dialogue. Naive transitivity is never totally and irrevocably surpassed; for all who enter the learning process, this remains a lifelong task.[23]

The final stage of critical consciousness, critical transitivity, is characterized by a person moving to a level of analysis that reveals the complexity of individual as well as institutional realities. Heaney summarizes:

> This stage is characterized by depth in the interpretation of problems, by testing one's own findings and openness to revision and reconstruction, by the attempt to avoid distortion when perceiving problems and to avoid preconceived notions when analyzing them, by rejecting passivity, by the practice of dialogue rather than polemics, by receptivity to the new without rejecting the old, and by permeable, interrogative, restless, and dialogical forms of life.[24]

Freire admits that these three categories are rough, broad, and not mutually exclusive or exhaustive. He also concedes that liberatory education is not the only way to engender critical consciousness in a potential social agent. The categories are, however, clear and powerful with regard to our overriding question as to what direction the Talented Tenth of tomorrow should take in energizing social change.

Ghosts on the Yard:
The Liberatory Challenge of the Talented Tenth

The restoration of black humanity and agency through the praxis of the Talented Tenth was, undoubtedly, what Du Bois had in mind at the turn of the twentieth century. He obviously believed the best start in this process was stimulating education and motivating teaching. While his praise of his instructors at Fisk is a testament to the fact that Du Bois understood the impact of good teaching (even though he himself is not reputed to have been good with students), it was Freire who engaged in examinations of structural pedagogical models that hampered student consciousness. As a result, Freire's liberatory education model makes it clear how education is linked to consciousness and the struggle for humanity. Liberatory education stands in stark contrast to the banking model that Freire decried as "maintaining and even stimulating the [teacher-student] contradiction . . . which mirrors oppressive society as a whole."[25]

Freire's contention that this model supports oppressive society by stripping students of any inclination to question and change the world is supported by Tom Heaney:

> [T]he practice of adult education in the United States has paralleled the advance of a technological society. Social, industrial, and political machines have similar needs. All require exchangeable parts, all need specialized components and tightly managed coordination. As technology has become more complex and specialized, so has schooling on all levels. Not only must skills be developed in bodies and minds, but attitudes must be formed which are supportive of a technological superstructure within which adult labor is organized.[26]

Such an educational design obviously leaves little room for questions or change. Whether contested terrains include racism, sexism, classism, or imperialism, alterations in the educational system are rarely accepted by society's controlling forces because such transformations threaten the very fabric of society itself. This is exactly what Du Bois felt the Talented Tenth should do: work to transform the world. Of course, attitudes concerning whether or not a society should be destroyed or preserved largely depend on whether one belongs to an oppressed or oppressive group.

Clearly, those who are most likely to question the discrepancies of society must be approached differently than those who are comfortable with the status quo. Therefore, strategies to condition members of disenfranchised groups in the society in such a way that questions are not asked and objective social, cultural, economic, and political contradictions are not realized or accentuated must be ever present. The more completely marginalized groups adapt to the purposes prescribed for them by core groups, the more easily the dominant group can maintain control through continued prescription. Freire concludes that the "theory and practice of banking education serve this end quite efficiently. Verbalistic lessons, reading requirements, the methods for evaluating 'knowledge,' the distance between the teacher and the taught, the criteria for promotion: everything in this ready-to-wear approach serves to obviate thinking."[27] Heaney once again supports Freire in this evaluation of the link between education and society:

> Even defenders of traditional schools have admitted that, if society is to hold together without the overt force of a police state, schooling must adapt learners to kinder, gentler controls: career choices (specialization), authority (dependency), and the good life (consumerism). Schooling must encourage competition (rule of the fittest), while maintaining order and cooperation (social conformism). As to the pursuit of happiness—in Jacques Ellul's words, "education makes us happy in a milieu which normally would make us unhappy, if we had not been worked on, molded, and formed for just that milieu.[28]

In contrast to this educational model that encourages passivity and conformity the liberatory model, from the outset, mandates that the teacher-student dichotomization be eradicated so that both are simultaneously teaching and taught. Without a doubt, many critics of Talented Tenth theory shun it because they believe the very idea of an intellectual elite reinforces, rather than destroys, the teacher-student divide. To a serious degree, they have been correct historically. The argument posed here, however, does not ignore this issue but seeks to focus attention on the real problem: the socialization and education of the Talented Tenth, not its mere existence.

This stance does not advocate undirected classroom chaos. It simply seeks to unify the teacher and student as cohorts in the humanization project that transcends lines of educational authority. The teacher must seek to transform himself or herself from an intellectual taskmaster into a partner of the students. They must become companions in a liberatory educational and political project that seeks to regain dominion over the creation and use of a material and immaterial culture that discovers and affirms that which is best in the black community. Only through such a process can they "better the world." Such amelioration is impossible without the critical consciousness produced by unyielding dialectical and dialogical engagement essential to the liberatory education of the Talented Tenth.

As we enter the twenty-first century, the struggle to transform the world continues, and the Talented Tenth must be involved. Our history teaches us that Du Bois was not wrongheaded when he posited that it is the educated who are most capable of actuating revolutionary change in American society. In order to engage in liberatory praxis, however, it is essential that the Talented Tenth not only have a deepseated understanding of American sociopolitical structures and culture but that they be absolutely dedicated to unselfishly challenging the systemic inequities of the society that marginalize the African-descended community.

Liberatory leaders have always been at the forefront of struggle. They must continue their integral role in bringing the humanization project to fruition. Liberatory leaders are mandatory, for it is they who give the masses a sense of who they are and who they can become. These are the people who encourage the development of critical consciousness by unlocking energies, imaginations, and minds. They pose compelling questions, clarify choices, explain options, teach reason, suggest possible directions, and urge us on in the face of disaster. These were the types of people Du Bois envisioned when he originally dreamed of the Talented Tenth. To be sure, not only did he theorize on how the Talented Tenth should benefit its community; he lived it.

Largely lost in many recollections of Du Bois is the fact that he almost single-handedly provided the model for what we now call the "organic intellectual" in black America. Even though Du Bois and others were already doing it, Sardinian philosopher Antonio Gramsci nicely articulated the charge of organic intellectualism. Gramsci maintained that social groups should generate their own distinct intellectuals whose work should always be grounded in the social and political struggles affecting that group beyond the walls of universities or the covers of books and journals. Gramsci and others believed this made sense because it was the intellectuals who were best equipped to examine complex issues involving their people. Without such an investment, Gramsci contended that much of the work of intellectuals was irrelevant.

Today, instead of holding true to Gramsci's stance that "groundedness" and active participation in group struggle are necessary to ensure intellectual work is meaningful, many scholars have chosen the role of uninvolved observer. William Banks believes Harvard African American Studies chairman Henry Louis Gates provides such an example. Without a doubt, Gates is a fine scholar. From personal experience, I also know he is an affable man. Banks, however, contends that Gates is antithetical to Du Bois and Gramsci's idea of the organic intellectual. He comments in *Black Intellectuals*, "Along with earlier idealists, Gates and many other scholars are interested in political matters, but in contrast to, say, Du Bois and Ralph Bunche, they want no part of the anxiety-ridden political process."[29] Gates makes the distinction between "doer and thinker" clear when he opines:

> I saw Khomeini come back from Paris. His return from exile was a very moving thing to behold. I thought he was wrong-headed and extreme. Still, it was very inspiring to see someone who's been in exile come back and take over. . . . You know he killed the giant through the force of an idea. I certainly don't mind being a part of something like that, but I want my role. . . . I'd rather watch it on a hill than be down there cheering the chief, because there are very few moments of which I could ever be an unambiguous part . . . I think about it too much.[30]

What such commentaries do not consider is the fact that ideas alone do not actuate sociopolitical change. Theories are beginnings, not ends. They must live and breathe through action. Du Bois, America's first black Harvard Ph.D., knew this and engaged in acting as well as thinking. From his involvement in the formation of the Niagara Movement and the NAACP to his masterful writings including *The Philadelphia Negro*, *Black Reconstruction*, *Dusk of Dawn*, and others, to his bold stands against Booker T. Washington, Du Bois dedicated himself to conceptualizing, organizing, and sustaining struggles against systemic repression. His ultimate mission was to mold himself into the most powerful organic intellectual possible, whose primary goal was creating American public space that blacks could enter without humiliation. This space would allow them to recognize themselves and also be recognized as viable people, not property or miserable beasts of burden existing slightly above the level of chattel. We should all be so dedicated. This dedication began for Du Bois at Fisk, was sharpened at Harvard, and continued throughout the remainder of his life.

Almost a century after Du Bois received his doctorate from Harvard, and seven decades after Charles Hamilton Houston served as the first black on the *Harvard Law Review*'s editorial board, Barack Obama became the *Law Review*'s first black president. This was no small feat.

> [Obama] was president of the *Harvard Law Review*, a position that requires not just the highest grades in the entire universe but also the unanimous acclaim of a band of viciously competitive law students and a famously divided faculty. Those who make *Law Review* are immediate stars, and fabulously fast-tracked. Those who have served on the *Law Review* include a stunning and stellar array of familiar names: Supreme Court Justices Felix Frankfurter, Ruth Bader Ginsburg, Antonin Scalia, Stephen Breyer and Chief Justice John Roberts; Dean Acheson, Alger Hiss, Archibald MacLeish, Judge Richard Posner, Michael Chertoff and New York Governor Eliot Spitzer. It is, in the secretly assigned world of global power, even a better ticket to the top than being sealed in a coffin at Skull and Bones. It was acknowledged as such when Jews first joined the *Law Review*, when Democratic political pundit Susan Estrich became the first woman president of the *Law Review* in 1976 and when Obama became its first black president.[31]

His time at Harvard clearly set Obama on his way. He may have had other important encounters outside his peers on the school's *Law Review*. You see, I believe schools have ghosts. The great institutions of our land are old, with their landmark buildings enduring the centuries. They have nurtured America's greatest minds. I often think of Martin Luther King Jr. walking the halls of Morehouse in the mid 1940s. Even though I entered the school four and a half decades later, I muse about the possibility—even the probability—that, at different times, our bodies inhabited the same physical space. I think King has spoken to me from time to time as I moved through those sacred places. I think he and other great Morehouse Men of the past speak to all Morehouse students. I believe King and our Morehouse brothers, along with other ghosts on campuses across the country, speak to students everywhere few of us listen. Many others do not.

Those who close their ears become the all-too-often encountered retrograde segment of today's black bourgeoisie. They are educated and talented, but they reject the responsibility of the Talented Tenth. As Du Bois lamented, they have the "single-minded idea, of seeing how much they [can] make out of [their educations] for themselves, and nobody else." Ultimately, many are damned to continuous doomed attempts to fill empty life spaces with more and more goods and organizational affiliations. They join and steep their identities in the Links and Boule. They send their children to Jack & Jill's to rub elbows with other affluent blacks while often excluding and condemning their less fortunate brothers and sisters. They walk around in false conscious funks, brains infested with the maggots of materialism—immersed in wine sips, ego trips, and political slips. "Give me more!" they silently scream into the expanse: more expensive cars, higher salaries, larger homes, more jewelry, more toys, more, more, more! Yes more, because "to have," indeed, is "to be." They gain things, but lose their humanity. They go to their megachurches but lose their souls. They did not listen to the ghosts on their yards.

Surely, just as King walks Morehouse's yard and speaks to its students, Du Bois and Houston linger at Harvard. I wonder if they spoke to Obama. I wonder if he felt their spirits, was infused with their energies, and was pushed forward by their sacrifices. Surely they spoke. The question is: Did Barack Obama listen?

3

The Witch and the Devil

American Political Philosophy and Black Suffering

> We must face the appalling fact that we have been betrayed
> by both the Democratic and Republican parties. The
> Democrats have betrayed us by capitulating to the whims
> and caprices of the Southern Dixiecrats. The Republicans
> have betrayed us by capitulating to the blatant hypocrisy of
> right-wing reactionary northerners.
> —Martin Luther King Jr., "Give Us the Ballot"

> The Democrats will kill us, but at least they'll wait 'til next
> week. The Republicans will do it tomorrow. We've just got
> to vote for survival—so we can fight another day.
> —Robert Douglas, University of Louisville Professor

When the smoke cleared after the hard-fought 2006 midterms, the Democrats stood victorious. Like the Republicans in 1994, Democrats had swept the opposition out of power and readied themselves to march triumphantly back to Capitol Hill, controlling both the House and the Senate. However, 2006 was different from 1994. At least three important factors caused many not to celebrate the Democrats' victory without apprehension. One, it was clear that voters were not necessarily wedded to the Democrats; they rejected the Republicans. Agree with them or not, the Gingrich-led Republicans had a discernible agenda embraced by a majority of voters in 1994. For good or ill, the goals of the "Contract with America" were clear. If the 1994 vote was one *for* the Republicans, the 2006 vote was definitely one *against* them.

Second, troubling for Americans tilted to the political Left, most of the Democrats elected were ideologically conservative or moderate. Very few, if any, stood out as trailblazers who would usher in a revolutionary political movement to shift the country left in the same way the GOP shifted it right with Reagan in 1980 or Gingrich in 1994. Finally, even in light of the far-reaching debauchery of the Republicans, most major races were very competitive. At the end of the day, any sincere analyst had to conclude the Democrats did not win the day; the Republicans lost it. After a veritable laundry list of missteps, the GOP still put up a fight. What did this say about the Democrats? What did it say about Americans? Beyond that, for those existing on the margins, did any of it really matter?

To be sure, in the midst of continued economic gain for a segment of America's population, large numbers of American citizens continue to bear the burden of creating and sustaining the flow of capital rather than enjoying it. Many societal incongruities are maintained, and even exacerbated, when engagements of these citizens' plights devalue and dichotomize racism and classism while never attacking institutional structures that foster both. While realizing that race and class certainly do not stand alone on America's contested terrains, if studied within the context of possible permanent American hegemony, they serve as cogent starting points for examination of the consequences of a ruling national ethos that wantonly commodifies anything and anyone.

The historical and contemporary debate as to whether economic greed created racism or vice-versa will certainly not be resolved in these pages. No matter which came first, both are now inseparably wedded within a degenerative political paradigm that nourishes American peripheralization. Those on the left who are serious about constructing oppositional struggles against such realities must be perennially aware that the problems of race and class are integral in the maintenance of American hegemony. The historical centrality of these two issues on the national landscape places them in a unique position from which they may help inform us on the possible progression of other marginalizing struggles that inhibit true sociopolitical and economic harmony. At their worst, America's social, economic, and political structures breed an environment of limited choice and manipulated consent in which marginalized citizens suffer but never ask the proper questions that may lead to the overhaul of agony-sustaining institutions. Many people do not question at all, because the system in which they reside has created a citizenry that nihilistically becomes disinterested in the issues affecting it.

People consequently acquiesce to their condition because they do not have access to what they see as viable political alternatives.

Prior to Election 2008, the general agreement that both George W. Bush and Albert Gore Jr. were, at best, mediocre presidential choices in 2000 and John Kerry was even worse in 2004 is evidence of this phenomenon on the individual level. The fact that no options to the present form of American capitalism are seriously discussed in the public arena is evidence of it on the institutional plane. Largely because of the lack of individual and institutional options, many citizens despair without hope for change. Even if one realizes that systemic repair is necessary and becomes interested in the complex realities that hold many Americans captive, he or she is often confused and ultimately neutered by a whirlwind of political constraint and convolution. These realities make the plotting of courses resistant to commodification and dehumanization difficult. To be fair, even Barack Obama may find it impossible to mend such a tattered fabric.

At this historical moment, radical black ideologues (and their compatriots across many lines of difference) must continue in their struggle to study and demystify oppressive systems and expand political dialogue beyond the traditional boundaries established by traditional liberals and conservatives. To that end, our discussion here revolves around three major themes. First of all, the difference between temporary and permanent hegemony—which necessarily entails social, political, and psychological repression—must be understood before any legitimate resistance movement can be organized or nurtured. Second, continued adherence to mainstream liberal and conservative political stances, both of which subscribe to the *philosophy of liberalism* and the capitalist system it has fostered and maintained, hamstring resistance discussions. Finally, in opposition to the tools and tactics used to sustain liberalism and the existing capitalist economic structure (e.g., the filtering of politics through popular culture and the cooptation of black elites), the Left must continuously seek to construct new approaches to politics and society that expose dominative institutions and doctrines. In doing so, we ultimately further the goals of the humanization project raised in the last chapter.

Understanding Permanent Hegemony and the Philosophy of Liberalism

When examining societal marginalization, Antonio Gramsci noted that hegemony and domination are not necessarily the same. Cultural and political studies have often invoked Gramsci's concept of 'hegemony' to describe moments of national sociopolitical struggle, but the term remains ambiguous to many. Probably the most common perception of hegemony sees it as a process through which domination of one group over another is achieved by constructing an ideological consensus.[1] This formulation of Gramsci is not altogether correct. A repeatedly ignored fact is that while hegemonic struggle always involves coercion and consent, it does not necessarily involve the negativity of domination.

A key variable in this political equation is power and how it is used. While power is necessary for domination to occur, domination and power are different in that power is not always negative. Unlike power, domination is marginalization marked by an exercise of supremacy over *and* oppression of another. This state is always retrograde. Hegemony, however, according to Gramsci, does not necessarily seek or equate to domination. He speaks of hegemony as having two faces by observing, "*Permanent* hegemony is always bad; *temporary* hegemony of one group or region may be beneficial to all. Hegemony of north over south in Italy has been bad but need not have been so."[2] From this perspective, temporary hegemony may result from positive leadership aimed at reaching some noble end for the collective. Permanent hegemony cannot be regarded as such.

If permanent hegemony in a sociopolitical space is established and maintained effectively, the ideas of the controlling class insinuate themselves into the lives of the oppressed to the point that subjugated people eventually do not regard themselves as worthwhile beings. Consequently, they base their worth on how well they mimic the behavior and life circumstances of the society's dominant group.[3] As Robert Owen and others have realized, "perverse social systems [such as this] create deformed human beings."[4] As previously observed, among the consequences of this reality are American obsessions with material gain, money, image, and gross consumerism rather than matters of the mind and human rights. To deploy Marx, the oppressor in a capitalist society believes that to have is to be, and the oppressed believe that to be is to be like the oppressor. Once such dehumanizing deformation takes effect, rehumanization of the masses can only take place through a deconstruction of oppressive institutions.

More often than not, capitalist preoccupations do not contest permanent hegemony or birth humanization. This is largely a result of the philosophy of liberalism that has driven American capitalism and politics since the country's inception. Modern liberalism, which emerged out of the Glorious Revolution of the seventeenth century, has enjoyed

a near ideological monopoly for most of American history.⁵ Bernard
Susser comments that liberalism initially "represented the revolt of a
rising urban middle class of merchants and entrepreneurs against the
pre-modern alliance of throne, sword, and altar—the absolute monar-
chy, the feudal aristocratic order, and the vast powers of the church."⁶
Ironically, liberalism has contributed to the development of an oppressive system of its own.

Simply stated, the philosophy espouses three basic values that
seem noble at first glance: individualism, freedom, and equality. Analysis of these core ideals, however, becomes complex when one examines
whether or not they are evenly distributed throughout American society. For instance, Lucius Barker, Mack Jones, and Katherine Tate have
argued that equality in American society is not automatically bestowed
upon all citizens. Equality actually has at least three aspects: political
(one person, one vote), social (individuals should not be treated
unfairly because of their station in life or circumstances of birth), and
legal (the law handles all citizens in the same manner). They assert that
these principles are so closely related that one cannot viably exist without the others. Therefore, if a person does not enjoy all three of these
equalities, he or she is not truly equal. Disturbingly, they conclude that
black Americans still have some distance to travel before these equalities are attained.⁷

Interestingly, liberalism helps to inhibit the realization of its own
ideals by setting boundaries of acceptable and unacceptable American
political behavior through the establishment of rarely deviated from
fundamental values and mores. Even though there are certainly those
who are right wing (commonly called "conservatives," who have a contemporary subgroup in modern political discourse—the neoconserva-
tives) and left wing (often referred to as "liberals" or "neo-liberals") relative to one another, in the context of American political ideology
they are all adherents to the same philosophy:

> To be sure, some American political activists prefer to be called
> conservatives. It is also true that the term liberal has come to be
> identified with the left branch of the liberal family tree. Neverthe-
> less, for the sake of historical and terminological accuracy it is
> important to understand that political debate in the United States
> takes place within a single tradition of ideological discourse: liber-
> alism. Strictly speaking, American conservatives and liberals are
> both liberals—estranged members of the same ideological family.
> Conservatives champion a position known as classical liberalism

while liberals support a more recent variant often described as welfare liberalism.[8] For all of their substantial differences, they remain
bound to a set of commonly accepted moral and political axioms.[9]

Within liberalism's "set of commonly accepted moral and political
axioms" are elements that should particularly concern oppressed populations. Among these worries are the principles of inequality and immo-
bility of income and wealth and the belief that economic deprivation is
a necessary stimulant for economic growth and development. Present-
day liberals never seriously seek to deconstruct the national economic
reality in which a minuscule segment of America's population controls
a disproportionately large share of the nation's income and wealth. This
discrepancy has remained relatively constant over time. Gabriel Kolko
writes that the top 10 percent of America's population received an economic amount equal to (or at times exceeding) the share received by the
bottom 50 percent through nearly the first two-thirds of the twentieth
century.[10] Others have commented that this trend continued through
the end of the century and "[more] recent reports suggest that changes
in this pattern are unlikely to occur in the foreseeable future."[11]

To exacerbate the problem of economic marginalization, liberalism
espouses the view that economic deprivation is an acceptable American reality. In arguing for the preeminence of individualism, liberals
purport that "government's primary responsibility is to create and safe-
guard conditions under which individual fulfillment can be pursued."[12]
It logically follows that in a supposedly individual-friendly, equal
opportunity environment, equal outcomes are achieved if equal effort
is given. If individuals do not work hard enough, they suffer. If they suffer enough, they will perform at a more competitive and productive
level. If a person is not successful within the system, his or her failure is
considered an individualistic flaw, not a systemic one. Thus, "liberal
philosophy (especially the classical variant) condones drastic income
inequality but depicts poverty and deprivation as the result of individual or group failure."[13]

Contesting this stance is the belief from the Left that the reality of
permanent hegemony and how it impacts marginalized people can be
evaluated from a perspective that calls the system, not individuals, into
question. For instance, there is no shortage of disturbing discrepancies
between blacks and whites in America. National statistics reveal that
black American males are five times more likely to serve time in jail or
prison than white men are. While black men make up between 5 and
6 percent of the country's population, they make up almost half of its

jail and prison population. The income of the average black family has never been more than 60 percent of what white families earn. As we entered the last decade of the twentieth century, whites' per capita wealth holdings averaged five times that of blacks.

At the same time, there was also a staggering 4 to 1 discrepancy between mean wealth holdings among whites and blacks. Even though the poverty rate for blacks reached its lowest level since 1959 in 1998, almost one-quarter of all blacks continue to live below the poverty line. A full one-third of all black children live in poverty. These are the highest rates of any single racial group in the country, including legally immigrated Hispanics. The black rate of poverty continues to be more than three times that of whites. The consistence, persistence, and occasional augmentation of gaps such as these would seem to indicate that there may be something more amiss than a lack of individual effort on the part of African American citizens.

Politics, the Personal, and the Popular: Maintaining Liberalism and Permanent Hegemony

American condemnation of the oppressed coupled with the almost unchecked competition and individualism of liberal philosophy opens the door for a dangerous brand of human interaction. The quest for money and materials becomes the center of many citizens' lives and mandates that they personally and collectively compromise themselves where issues of structural political change and true equality are concerned. It follows that American institutions and leaders who claim to speak to and for the masses, but are committed to the maintenance of capitalist class and racial balkanization, must necessarily be called into question. In the absence of such challenges, permanent hegemony and societal contradictions endure no matter who wins various parochial political squabbles or presidential elections. Admittedly, such confrontation is difficult in a political environment sanitized and dumbed by the filtering of the political through popular culture and the visceral, underdeveloped, pseudopolitical engagement bred by it. If productive dialogical exchange and clear articulation of issues and agendas *within* liberal space rarely occur, it is almost impossible to alter society into a site of political struggle that is systemically oppositional by presenting alternative possibilities from without.

Some would argue that the appearance of George W. Bush and Albert Gore on a spate of television talk shows ranging from *David*

Letterman to *Queen Latifah* (yes, she had a television show) during the 2000 campaign for the American presidency was an attempt to enlighten and politicize the electorate. Contrarily, one could also argue that such a use of popular media did just the opposite. To be sure, the television shows served to mobilize support for each candidate, but they also had an unspoken purpose and effect. More important than their contribution to an individual's decision to vote for Bush or Gore was the fact that media served as a vehicle which helped establish (at least partial) consent of these same people by popular rearticulation of liberal agendas in terms which did not seem hegemonic at all. Indeed, Lawrence Grossberg has commented, "hegemony always involves a struggle to rearticulate the popular":[14]

> Hegemonic leadership has to operate where people live their lives. It has to take account of and even allow itself to be modified by its engagement with the fragmentary and contradictory terrain of common sense and popular culture. This is where the social imaginary is defined and changed; where people construct personal identities, identifications, priorities and possibilities; where people form and formulate moral and political agendas for themselves and societies. . . . Speaking in the vocabulary of popular ideologies, using the logics by which people attempt to calculate their most advantageous position, celebrating the pleasures of popular culture, appropriating the practices of daily life—this is where hegemony is fought and what it is fought over.[15]

Often, rearticulation of (and through) the popular is not a true political articulation at all. It is, quite contrarily, an appeal to more personal, emotive factors that have little (if anything) to do with hegemonic struggle, the transformation of the world, or (at its worst—or best—depending on one's perspective) politics. Certainly, the elevation of support for Gore in some quarters after the 2000 Democratic National Convention, because he engaged in a long, passionate kiss with his wife, had little to do with political struggle. With respect to style over substance, however, Bush is possibly a better example than Gore. While Green Party candidate Ralph Nader criticized both major party nominees and labeled them as "interchangeable," it is probably accurate to conclude that Gore (and later, Kerry) was indeed to the left of Bush in some respects and definitely the more astute politician. Beyond this admission, and contrary to Nader's attempt to characterize himself as such, it would be flawed to argue that either Gore or Nader was a thinker *on the left* if the Left is in fact the ideological camp that seeks to dismantle American liberalism and capitalism in their present forms.

All of these men were ultimately liberals to one degree or another and never conceptualized that structural change that confronts the permanent hegemony of capitalism is necessary. Unlike Nader, Gore, or Kerry, Bush openly conducted his campaigns as the conservative, classical liberal member of the family, and much of his early support centered on romanticized notions of him as a potentially unifying force for America. This nonpolitical concentration on the personal and the popular is not a strange phenomenon in the context of the new classical liberalism:

> A number of features of the new conservatism, especially when taken together, offer a perplexing scenario. First, and perhaps most important, the new conservative formations seem to have broadly based popular and emotional appeal. Second, this appeal is often quite distinct from popular support for the specific programs and positions of the new conservatism, although such support is often mobilized and orchestrated.[16] Third, there is often an obvious contradiction between the new conservatism's explicitly stated projects and its actions (e.g. its anti-statist project of deconstructing the social-democratic compromise of the postwar years versus its reconstruction of powerful politically aligned state apparatuses; its rhetoric of economic prosperity versus the real economic devastation resulting from its policies; and its rhetoric of individual liberty versus its "war" on civil liberties). Fourth, this formation is able to win the electoral support of class fractions which would seem to have strong reasons to oppose the interests and policies of the new conservatives.[17]

To the detriment of political engagement, an inordinate amount of debate in both the Bush-Gore and Bush-Kerry elections centered on which candidates were more likable. The discussions, at many junctures, mutated into ones that seemed to mull over who would be a more intriguing dinner guest rather than who would be a more competent president. Such flurries of political confusion compound marginalization in America in general and among blacks in particular. Often, the direction of the black vote is dictated by a decision on which candidate will damage them the least rather than which will speak to their interests the most. Such a political climate breeds a rightly deserved lack of trust among peripheralized people. As much as liberal and conservative politicians claim to detest one another's political stances, a percentage of blacks have slowly grown to realize that both support the maintenance of the same system.

Elite Cooptation and Exploitation:
The Failure of Black Leadership

It is difficult to deny that a dichotomized oppressor-oppressed society has been established when America's historical and contemporary discrepancies along numerous cleavages within liberal structures are examined. If it is conceded (and many people certainly do not) that this dehumanizing reality does indeed exist, then the primary concern for members of the oppressed group must be the restoration of humanity. As Du Bois argued, quality analysis, understanding, and commitment are essential in such endeavors. Unfortunately, on many fronts, current black American leadership falls short.

Among black politicians, for example, the fight against oppression is frustrated by their cooptation into long-standing ideological groups that marginalize the masses. Like core-group liberal politicians, most black elected officials believe pluralism is the most legitimate tool for political advancement. In taking this position, they advocate that the American policy-making process rests on a base of multiple centers of power to which all adversely affected groups have the opportunity to present their cases at some point in the decision-making process. Ideally, constituencies' needs are met, because they can access different centers of power if others do not satisfy them. Through this process marked by bargaining, negotiation, and the formation of political coalitions and alliances, all groups play a role in public policy resolutions.[18]

Like liberalism, pluralism has a number of problems. First of all, while some citizens have retreated from the political process altogether, those who remain involved do not completely participate in final decision making, because many issues of local and national import lie outside boundaries of politics proper as a result of the growing power of special interest groups. The issues these groups influence with the infusion of capital into the political process ultimately place them out of the reach of truly democratic processes. Remember Jack Abramoff? Pluralists also never consider the possibility that not only is the idea of perennially open access points to the system mythical, but as the Left purports, the system itself may be flawed. One of the most telling facts that the American system of governance is marginalizing can be located in the observation that even though the number of black elected officials has increased substantially since the 1960s, vast discrepancies remain between blacks and whites socially, economically, and politically:

Although blacks constitute 11 percent of the nation's voting-age population, less than 2 percent of all elected officials in the nation are black. In 1995, according to the Joint Center for Political and Economic Studies, there were more than 8,500 black elected officials nationwide, a total over 5 times greater than the number in 1970.[19] Almost half of these officials served at the municipal level, and slightly more than one-fifth served on school boards. Also of interest is the geographical breakdown of these officials. Seventeen states in 1993 had higher percentages of black voting-age residents than the national average of 11 percent, yet in only five states (Georgia, Alabama, Mississippi, Louisiana, and South Carolina) did blacks constitute more than 10 percent of the elected officials.[20]

For the most part, blacks continue to be locked out of the most important political positions in the land. Albert Gore's selection of conservative Democrat (now Independent) Joseph Lieberman (an orthodox Jew) as his vice-presidential running mate in 2000, which was regarded by some observers as a landmark move toward true inclusivity, without seriously considering a person of African descent for the post reflects this truth. Before Barack Obama's candidacy, earnest discussion of a black running for and *winning* the presidency was far-fetched. Even with Obama's landmark run, race still plays a prominent role in American politics:

> Despite signs of progress, blacks have yet to achieve political power commensurate with their numbers. For blacks to reach proportionality in elected office and, more specifically, for blacks to increase their membership in Congress, it seems clear that more whites will have to start voting for black candidates. . . . [P]olling data indicates that white voters generally consider blacks less capable of achieving goals, less likely to possess important personal attributes, and less qualified for higher political offices than whites. In addition, a majority of whites surveyed agreed that most whites vote on the basis of race rather than qualifications.[21]

Considering these studies, as well as the reality that blacks' participation in the electoral process continues to decline, and nearly 15 percent of all black males in the country have lost their right to vote because of felony convictions, alternate political approaches are now mandatory.[22]

Serious analysis of the black human condition, from politics to poverty, forces one to make the admission that current paradigms do little to alleviate their suffering. Disturbingly, not only do the models presently in use (as well as the leaders who promote them) not seriously contest repression, but they also aid in anesthetizing liberatory praxis among the masses. One of Manning Marable's more powerful critiques of black leadership in the 1980s is still fitting:

> Their [black leadership's] failure, in brief, is one of vision. The Old Guard constantly maneuvers, responding to minor political crises, but they are hopelessly inept in projecting a constructive program to transform the larger society. They react, rather than act; they imitate rather than create; they plead rather than demand. Theirs is a failure within a qualified and compromised success, and as the decade of the 1980s progresses, it has become obvious that the result of their limited vision has been the creation of a temporary yet quite real barrier between the immediate political agenda of the elite and the black majority. With Du Bois, I must agree that many critical failures of both Reconstructions were the result of black leadership "by the blind." We fell under the leadership of those who would compromise with truth in the past in order to make peace in the present and guide policy in the future.[23]

Even though Marable saw the gap between elites and the masses as "temporary" in the 1980s, in many respects the problem worsened, rather than improved, as the twentieth century ended.

In response to this situation, the radical ideologue must—in concert—question and challenge oppressive economic and political institutions. To be sure, such oppositions are difficult to inject into the public arena of discourse and debate, because permanently hegemonic systems maintain themselves by leaving as little room as possible for real question or change. Alterations to the management of such a society's citizenry are not accepted if they challenge the systems rather than singular aspects of them. Because they threaten to transform the fabric of a society itself, structural confrontations are usually not tolerated. Understandably, at the end of the day, attitudes concerning whether or not a society should be destroyed or preserved are largely dependent upon whether one belongs to a marginalized or privileged group.

Ultimately, change in systems designed to maintain permanent hegemony of the few over the many does not come from consent, but dissent. As Saul Alinsky proclaimed, the question most often asked by any radical spirit is, "Why?"[24] Ultimately, the point of such questioning and the end goal of radicalism must be the restoration (or introduction) of American humanity, which can only occur if real analyses of the effects of capitalism and liberal philosophy take place. The overarching problem that plagues black leadership (political or otherwise) is that many of them aspire to enjoy the fruits of capitalist bourgeois elite life themselves. Consequently, when faced with the reality that the only course of action that may alleviate black suffering is the dismantling of hegemonic capitalist structures, they balk. Marable makes another cogent point when he proclaims:

> The ideological limitations impressed upon black thought and politics during the Cold War are still operative upon the current black leadership. The black elite will promulgate an economic program which mirrors the right-wing tendencies of Social Democracy in most of the Western world's nations, but beyond that invisible boundary, they will go no further left. In short, the black elite calls for federal initiatives to provide employment for the poor, but will not advocate a clearly socialist agenda which would severely restrict the prerogatives of private capital. They denounce the growing trend of racist violence, but they will not see that such violence is a manifestation of a more profound crisis within the capitalist political economy. . . . They are simply ready to administer the crisis, but are ill-prepared to resolve it.[25]

Ultimately, across lines of race, capitalism's bourgeois elites conspire (sometimes unknowingly) to maintain hegemonic dynamics that stifle the humanization of oppressed populations. A good percentage of black leadership has reached a historical moment in which it seemingly no longer seeks to liberate or transform the world but languishes in vulgar careerism and selfishness that reinforce, rather than oppose, American peripheralization. Leadership will only be effective and liberatory if populated by men and women who are seriously committed to forming oppositional movements that alleviate the effects of exploitation on various fronts. To be sure, the call here is for no less than the identification, rejection, and replacement of black leadership that is not dedicated to such a mission. The question for Barack Obama is, On which side of this struggle will he find a home?

4

"Black Hawks" Down

America's War on Terror and the Rise of Bushism

> Somewhere tonight men in powerful positions are taking the first steps toward sending our country to war. Somewhere tonight powerful interests are working to silence those that are a threat to their power.
>
> —Congresswoman Cynthia McKinney, Concession Speech after loss to Denise Majette (August 21, 2002)

Three weeks before the first anniversary of the September 11 attacks, Georgia congresswoman Cynthia McKinney was defeated in the Democratic primary by political upstart Denise Majette.[1] This marked the possible culmination of a slow but important shift in black America's political leadership community. Much was written about this race. Most arguments from the Left contextualized it as an election that heralded a number of disturbing realities for black politics. First of all, McKinney's bid for reelection to a sixth term was largely trumped by the infusion of large amounts of money into Majette's campaign by Jewish Americans and other Israeli supporters from outside her district—many outside of Georgia altogether—who saw her as unfriendly to Israel.[2] This was clearly the result of McKinney's criticism of former New York mayor Rudolph Guliani's refusal to accept money from an Arab dignitary following September 11 and subsequent vocal support of Palestinian independence and freedom from what she saw as Israeli aggression.

The shoring up of Majette's political war chest by pro-Israeli individuals and interest groups motivated by a single, external issue not directly related to the problems and concerns in the candidates' district raised the ire of some black politicians and laypeople alike. Texas representative and congressional Black Caucus chairwoman Eddie Bernice Johnson commented immediately following McKinney's defeat:

> I definitely have some feelings about any outside group exerting this kind of influence in a race, and I've been receiving angry calls from black voters all day saying they should rally against Jewish candidates. To have non-African Americans from around the country putting millions into a race to unseat one of our leaders for expressing her right of free speech is definitely a problem.[3]

Second, McKinney's defeat by a much more rhetorically moderate Majette raised the possibility that black politicians who "talk black" were falling out of favor. Just as some politicians who strongly advocate war have historically been called "War Hawks," I believe black politicians such as McKinney who often speak to issues of race can be accurately labeled 'Black Hawks.' The Yale- and Duke-educated Majette, whom some characterized as a Republican in Democratic clothing, may very well be typical of what the black politician may look like on a political and social landscape marked by racial anaesthetization.

People such as former Tennessee "Blue Dog" congressman Harold Ford Jr. and Newark mayor Corey Booker epitomize this new breed of centrist, let-us-not-rock-the-boat Democrats. Ford and Booker are not alone in this group, and the question as to whether or not they will soon displace the old Black Hawks is pressing. Washington lobbyist and Democratic fund-raiser Jarvis Stewart opines, "The black electorate is increasingly well-educated, more entrepreneurial, business-savvy and politically moderate. Many who were not raised in the era of the Civil Rights Movement don't relate to or see the benefit in polarizing politics."[4] In other words, the Black Hawks have out-lived their usefulness. Many argue that Barack Obama also fits comfortably into this new category of relatively harmless post–civil rights black politicians.

Without a doubt, McKinney's greatest problems stemmed from her criticism of George Bush after September 11. Her assertions that the Bush administration had knowledge of the bombings that it did not disclose, prompted a wave of criticism across racial lines from moderates as well as those on the right. Democratic pollster Ron Lester commented on McKinney, "Black voters are as emotional about 9/11 as any other voters. They were happy with the way she served the district, but a certain segment of black voters were very wary of her remarks and the controversy surrounding her."[5] McKinney's own camp was clear on where it stood with relation to their Black Hawk's image in comparison to the "safe" Majette's. McKinney campaign worker Alfreida Capers submitted:

> People in the black community still think of the comments she made after 9/11, and they are still a little apprehensive. There were some in our community who saw Ms. Majette's advertisements on television and thought they reflected a young, Christian woman with a family who would be less boisterous and they carried that thought with them to the polls.[6]

If there was apprehension in the black community toward McKinney, many in the white community displayed outright hostility.[7] Primary elections in the state of Georgia are "open," which means members of one party can vote in the other party's primary. Even though voting in the opposing party's primary prohibits voters from participating in their own party's election, in a district where Republican competition is almost a nonfactor, a relatively large number of Republicans crossed over and voted for Majette. Sentiment that bordered on personal hatred for McKinney was commonly encountered among Republican voters. One woman actually refused to speak McKinney's name during an interview, "I switched over today for one person to beat another. I just don't like her [McKinney] at all."[8] Another self-proclaimed "50-year Republican" exclaimed, "If I could vote a thousand times against her, I would." In a rather feeble attempt to soften the rather personal tone of his stance, this voter proclaimed that he did not dislike McKinney personally, but "I hate her politics. . . . I'm willing to do everything in my power to keep her from being elected."[9]

Loving America the "Right" Way

As troubling as the circumstances surrounding McKinney's fall were, it is even more important to understand that what she, former Alabama representative Earl Hilliard, and others were swept into was a wave of xenophobia that marked American social interaction and politics after September 2001.[10] In the post-September 11 political arena, any dialogical engagements that did not center on terrorist attacks or Middle Eastern and/or Arab hatred of America were all but forgotten. This changed radically as more Americans died in Iraq, and the situation became increasingly untenable in the next half-decade. However, in the initial years after September 11 American politics were driven by the antithesis of the sentiment leading to the Democratic overthrow of 2006.

In the immediate post–September 11 political environment, any attempt to raise questions around issues negatively affecting blacks was viewed as ill-timed at best and treasonous at worst. In this new age of xenophobic American nationalism and war-mongering disguised as defensive protection against a new "evil empire" (which the President Bush dubbed the "axis of evil"), American politics and politicians expanded popular space for rhetorical and literal flag waving and song rather than real engagement of continuing domestic ills and retrograde foreign policy that unleashed yet another barrage of bombing campaigns on another already suffering country: Afghanistan.

Congress then gave the president authority to unleash American military force on Iraq once again. For years after September 11, balanced discussion of the impetus, implications, and consequences of the attacks in New York City and Washington, D.C., were not achieved. That dialogical space for conversation on this issue has been expanded cannot be denied, even though it is still contested. In the days immediately following the attacks, freedom of speech in America reached a nadir for our generation. If one did not subscribe to the party line of ultrapatriotism and the necessary shortsighted dichotomization that accompanied it (which painted the engagement as a battle between absolute good and evil), one's opinion was often muted. The reality of the situation was that most Americans, no matter their racial or ethnic background, who did not buy the self-righteous American spin, lock, stock, and barrel were not willing to voice their evaluations of the national drama with global implications lest they be painted by twenty-first-century McCarthyites as disloyal and deserving of death.

Many reasonable people were disturbed by the almost spontaneous mutation of otherwise (seemingly) rational Americans into angry fanatics calling for the immediate destruction—by bomb, bullet, or blade—of anyone who uttered a negative word about the United States. People suddenly became proud citizens who loudly adopted the age-old conservative adage, "America—love it or leave it." This was an interesting development indeed, especially when such words of vehemence and loyalty dripped from the lips of blacks, who have been the victims of various forms of domestic terrorism for centuries. Many even invoked the family analogy to describe black-white American unification on the matter. As the line of reasoning went, we may pick on family members, but if an outsider seeks to join in on the fun, he has hell to pay.

No longer did it matter what America's historical and current internal transgressions along lines of race, ethnicity, class, sex, or anything else were. In the wake of the "United We Stand" feel-good sentiment following the atrocities, even George W. Bush and Rudolph Giuliani, who had been considered callous at best and inept at worst just a week earlier, were suddenly deified and regarded as strong leaders. Giuliani was able to transform this momentum into a short-lived Republican front-runner position early in the 2008 presidential campaign. All was forgiven, and everyone was bonded around a common mission, a new "War on Terror." This endeavor united Americans in figuring out a way to dispel the vile Middle Eastern/Arab/Muslim terrorist threat and anyone who supported it (or resembled it). The persecution and murder of innocent American citizens of Middle Eastern descent on campuses and in communities around the country in the days following the bombings was evidence of this sentiment reaching a frenzied extreme in some quarters.[11] This certainly must be considered carefully when one notes that no random attacks on whites took place after Timothy McVeigh's actions in Oklahoma City.

To combat this phenomenon of nonrational-critical thought, segments of the Left were consistent—even though their volume has certainly crescendoed and fell to pianissimo from time to time—in contextualizing debates on the September 11 attacks. The most effective analyses of the dilemma considered, though were not necessarily limited to, three major concerns: issues of humanity, security, and policy. Most people believe the attacks of September 11 were wrong and unjustifiable. No right-thinking person can say the deaths of thousands of people were warranted or deserved. No serious commentary from the American Right or Left has taken such an indefensible stand. The very thought of innocent fathers, mothers, sisters, brothers, sons, and daughters who were simply attempting to work and earn a living dying en masse will be disturbing far beyond September 11. It would be difficult to make this a case of individual Americans reaping what they had sown, though the institutional issue is another one altogether.[12] On the microindividual level though, the occupants of the World Trade Center were, more than likely, not among those who sow national and global policy seeds that reap anything good or bad.

To be sure, innocent working people suffered the most in this attack, the common, everyday folk who struggle to make ends meet in an effort to enjoy the elusive American Dream. But, in the aftermath of this event, one must remember that the wanton loss of innocent life anywhere should be condemned, whether in New York, Washington, Kabul, Baghdad, Kosovo, Nairobi, Dar es Salaam, or Havana. Americans would do well to remember that loss of life is often the result of a loss of conscience. They should therefore reflect on the contradictions when they are angered to violence by loss of life on American soil but feel absolutely nothing when viewing the consistent loss of human life around the globe, sometimes as a consequence of American actions.

While there was almost nonstop talk targeting Osama bin Laden as the mastermind behind the September 11 attacks, there was very little discussion of the fact that America financed bin Laden and many of his kind during Afghanistan's struggle against the Soviet Union for nearly a decade in the 1980s. During this time, bin Laden was not regarded as a terrorist by the American government (even though he was engaged in the same types of activities); he was dubbed a "noble freedom fighter." If Osama bin Laden was wrong on September 11 (and if he did orchestrate the attacks, most people agree that he was wrong), then was he not wrong when he levied the same type of terror (given, on a smaller scale) on Soviet citizens? When considering the human factor, one must be mindful that—contrary to the views of a percentage of America's population—innocent human beings who have nothing to do with terrorism do indeed exist outside the United States. Are their lives worth less than those of American citizens?

Though it has diminished as we move farther away from September 11, many still fear something swift and terrible may befall them, their families, or their friends at any moment. In this regard, the terrorists were quite successful. By targeting not only military sites, the attackers birthed the mind-set that anyone and anywhere is fair game in this "new war." Everyone is concerned about this issue to some degree. The Sniper killings in Washington, D.C., Maryland, and Virginia in October 2002 and the Virginia Tech massacre in April 2007 helped augment this fear. In spite of these realities, one can be vigilant regarding security issues without transforming into a superpatriot who mindlessly waves American flags or tries to run down Middle Eastern women in the streets of New York while screaming, "You're destroying my country," as one American did in the days immediately following September 11. We can be concerned about security and not force Middle Eastern citizens off airplanes as three men were from a Northwest Airlines flight to Salt Lake City, Utah, on September 19, 2001. We can be concerned about security without becoming absolutely unconcerned about the preservation of civil liberties, which supposedly sit at the heart of this nation.

As Americans watched the country's news outlets, which—intentionally or unintentionally—worked the citizenry's patriotism and anger to a feverish pitch, serious sociopolitical engagement of September 11 was all but lost. The charge was led by Fox News, but others were not far behind. In the name of security, insensitive, fanatical madness from our own ranks took hold of the airwaves. Below are a few examples:

> *Bill O'Reilly:* "If the Taliban government of Afghanistan does not cooperate, then we will damage that government with air power, probably. All right? We will blast them, because . . ."
>
> *Sam Husseini, Institute for Public Accuracy:* "Who will you kill in the process?"
>
> *O'Reilly:* "Doesn't make any difference."
>
> —(*The O'Reilly Factor*, Fox News Channel, September 13, 2001)

> This is no time to be precautious about locating the exact individuals directly involved in this particular terrorist attack. . . . We should invade their countries, kill their leaders and convert them to Christianity. We weren't punctilious about locating and punishing only Hitler and his top officers. We carpet-bombed German cities; we killed civilians. That's war. And this is war.
>
> —Syndicated columnist Ann Coulter
> (*New York Daily News*, September 12, 2001)

> There is only one way to begin to deal with people like this, and that is you have to kill some of them even if they are not immediately directly involved in this thing.
>
> —Former secretary of state Lawrence Eagleburger
> (CNN, September 11, 2001)

> The response to this unimaginable 21st-century Pearl Harbor should be as simple as it is swift—kill the bastards. A gunshot

between the eyes, blow them to smithereens, poison them if you have to. As for cities or countries that host these worms, bomb them into basketball courts.

—Steve Dunleavy (*New York Post*, September 12, 2001)

America roused to a righteous anger has always been a force for good. States that have been supporting, if not Osama bin Laden, people like him need to feel pain. If we flatten part of Damascus or Tehran or whatever it takes, that is part of the solution.

—Rich Lowry, *National Review* editor to Howard Kurtz (*Washington Post*, September 13, 2001)

Unfortunate for rational-critical debate, these statements displayed American sentiment that was limited at best—arrogant and foolish at worst. As many feared in the immediate aftermath of the September 11 attacks, they served as catalysts for political, social, and economic xenophobes to take center stage without challenge or shame. The American political landscape has yet to completely recover from the consequences. What brought September 11 about and how America would respond were the most important questions considered in the months immediately following the event. The Black Radical Congress issued a statement following the bombings that, while condemning the September attacks, made the point that American foreign policy was not always viewed as benevolent:

It is without question that U.S. imperialism has brought genocidal levels of death and destruction to people around the world. Whether one looks at the situation in Iraq with the continual blockade and air bombardments, the situation in Palestine where the U.S. continues to give virtually uncritical support to the Israelis in their national oppression of the Palestinians, the economic blockade against Cuba which aims to undermine its economy and weaken its population, or any number of other places, one clearly sees the callousness and evil intent with which U.S. imperialism treats the lives and property of others, especially non-white peoples around the globe.[13]

On the day of the attacks, MIT linguist Noam Chomsky, who is no stranger to dissent, released a brief dispatch entitled "On the Bombings" and made the following comments:

The terrorist attacks were major atrocities. In scale they may not reach the level of many others, for example, Clinton's bombing of the Sudan with no credible pretext, destroying half its pharmaceutical supplies and killing unknown numbers of people (no one knows, because the U.S. blocked an inquiry at the UN and no one cares to pursue it). Not to speak of much worse cases, which easily come to mind. But that this was a horrendous crime is not in doubt. The primary victims, as usual, were working people: janitors, secretaries, firemen, etc. It is likely to prove to be a crushing blow to Palestinians and other poor and oppressed people. It is also likely to lead to harsh security controls, with many possible ramifications for undermining civil liberties and internal freedom.[14]

Chomsky's prediction that forces arrayed against Palestine would be augmented was accurate. His foretelling of the curtailing of domestic civil liberties also proved correct. At the Bush administration's behest, bills were either passed or considered that gave the president, Attorney General John Ashcroft, Secretary of Defense Donald Rumsfeld, and others near carte blanche with such matters as augmentations in defense budgeting, phone tapping, video surveillance, as well as detention and deportation "discretion" when dealing with those suspected of terrorist affiliation.[15] One suggestion went so far as to posit that, in the name of "homeland security," Attorney General Ashcroft should have the ability to detain and deport suspected terrorists without presenting solid evidence that the individuals were, in fact, terrorists.

Of course, this approach was ill-fated. By 2005, John Ashcroft was gone. Immediately following the 2006 Democratic election wins, Bush replaced the long-embattled Rumsfeld. By mid-2007, most Americans had soured on the Iraqi War, Bush's approval rating had dropped into the thirtieth percentile, and Democratic leaders were accusing him of behaving more like a king than a president. As fall 2007 approached, the "Architect," Karl Rove, announced he would leave Bush's administration. A few weeks later, Ashcroft's embattled successor, Alberto Gonzalez, also offered his resignation and made his long-called-for exit. Bush's age of "cowboy diplomacy" seemed to be coming to an end. Unfortunately, his policies had taken on lives of their own.

Hubris and its consequences were not limited to Bush and his loyalists. Well beyond September 11 many Americans asked, "Why do people around the globe hate us?" Some of the answers could be found as close as the rather sanctimonious reasons given for foreign disdain by American commentators immediately following the bombings that were long forgotten by 2007:

> [The World Trade Center and the Pentagon] have drawn, like gathered lightning, the anger of the enemies of civilization. Those enemies are always out there. . . . Americans are slow to anger but mighty when angry, and their proper anger now should be alloyed with pride. They are targets because of their virtues—principally democracy, and loyalty to those nations which, like Israel, are embattled salients of our virtues in a still-dangerous world.
>
> —George Will (*Washington Post*, September 12, 2001)

> This nation symbolizes freedom, strength, tolerance, and democratic principles dedicated to both liberty and peace. To the tyrants, the despots, the closed societies, there are no alterations to the policies, no gestures we can make, no words we can say that will convince those determined to continue their hate.
>
> —Charles G. Boyd (*Washington Post*, September 12, 2001)

> Are Americans afraid to face the reality that there is a significant portion of this world's population that hates America, hates what freedom represents, hates the fact that we fight for freedom worldwide, hates our prosperity, hates our way of life? Have we been unwilling to face that very difficult reality?
>
> —Sean Hannity (Fox News Channel, September 13, 2001)

> Our principled defense of individual freedom and our reluctance to intervene in the affairs of states harboring terrorists makes us an easy target.
>
> —Robert McFarlane (*Washington Post*, September 13, 2001)

Just as most of us can be sure the attacks of September 11 were wrong and reprehensible, we can also be sure that many people around the globe see America as villain, not savior. All of them probably do not "hate freedom" or are intrinsically "evil" as some American leaders would have the country believe. Neither are all of them members of Al-Qaeda, Hamas, or Islamic Jihad. Is it possible that there is something about American foreign policy that may need revisiting? Could it be that, contrary to what some believe, we have room for growth—to be more caring, more just, more human? Chomsky ends "On the Bombings" with appropriate words when he remarks:

> As to how to react, we have a choice. We can express justified horror; we can seek to understand what may have led to the crimes, which means making an effort to enter the minds of the likely perpetrators. If we choose the latter course, we can do no better, I think, than to listen to the words of Robert Fisk, whose direct knowledge and insight into affairs of the region is unmatched after many years of distinguished reporting. Describing "The wickedness and awesome cruelty of a crushed and humiliated people," he writes that "this is not the war of democracy versus terror that the world will be asked to believe in the coming days. It is also about American missiles smashing into Palestinian homes and U.S. helicopters firing missiles into a Lebanese ambulance in 1996 and American shells crashing into a village called Qana and about a Lebanese militia—paid and uniformed by America's Israeli ally—hacking and raping and murdering their way through refugee camps." And much more. Again, we have a choice: we may try to understand, or refuse to do so, contributing to the likelihood that much worse lies ahead.[16]

The September 11 Frontier and the Rise of Bushism

In light of this latest sociopolitical directed massification of Americans, a revisitation of Lawrence Grossberg's engagement of the relationship between the political and the popular is fruitful:

> In a hegemonic struggle . . . the social field cannot be easily divided into two competing groups. The diversity of "the people" confounds any such simple divisions; for while the masses appear to be undifferentiated, social differences actually proliferate. The difference between the subordinate and the dominant cannot be understood on a single dimension. Power has to be organized along many different, analytically equal axes: class, gender, ethnicity, rage, age, etc., each of which produces disturbances in the others. At the same time, those seeking to hold the dominant position do not constitute a single coherent group or class. Instead, a specific alliance of class fractions, a "bloc" which must already have significant economic power, attempts to win a position of leadership by re-articulating the social

and cultural landscape and their position within it. This re-articulation is never a single battle. It is a continuous "war of positions" dispersed across the entire terrain of social and cultural life. At each site, in each battle, the "ruling bloc" must re-articulate the possibilities and recreate a new alliance of support which places it in the leading position. It must win, not consensus, but consent.[17]

It follows that the ruling bloc is not static and realizes it must constantly appeal to the masses by articulating and rearticulating what is good and proper as often as possible. No matter how much their rhetoric seems to change, however, it always caters to a perspective that includes some notion that they are making a dynamic and healthy shift to a stable set of ideals invariably rooted in the past. In this respect, current American nationalist ideologues are taking a page out of Britain's political handbook. Of course, this has often been the case. To paraphrase Northern Ireland's Shin Fein president Gerry Adams: Americans have always had good relations (which include mimicry) with the British once they forced the British out of America.

In recent history, one can certainly examine the political rise of Margaret Thatcher in Britain as reflective of an appeal to the popular where ideals, stability, and threat are concerned.[18] The driving force behind "Thatcherism" was its ability to identify an "enemy within," which threatened the very existence of good "Englishness."[19] Of course, in order to make this appeal to the society and cause lines of division that augmented Thatcher's political power in English society, she had to present to the public what she felt this ideal "Englishness" was or had been. What happened in reality was Thatcher created an emotion-filled myth that appealed to the masses. Eventual adherence to a false history of what engendered English greatness, stability, and morality carried paranoid side effects such as racism and classism along with it, because there must be reasons for the loss of mythic prosperity and peace. One cannot ignore the historical reality that this was the same strategy used by Fascists in Germany but with much more extreme results.

This is also the case with the current brand of American conservatism and nationalism that I am hesitant to but will go forward in labeling "Bushism." In Bushist philosophy, as with the paradigms forwarded by Reagan and Bush the Father, the reasons for the loss of mythic America magically change over time. They shift from external (the Russian threat [the original evil empire], Gaddafi, Hussein, bin

Laden, Kim Jong Il, Mahmoud Ahmadinejad, Middle Eastern terrorists in general, or the United Nations' lack of backbone with regard to sanction enforcement on Iraq) to internal (affirmative action, welfare policy, the deviancy of homosexuals, lack of public and financial support for our military, or Congress' reluctance to give the president unchecked war-making powers) depending upon the national crisis at hand. Even cursory examination reveals the fact that the progression of conservative strategy, Bushism included, does not change. Conservatives move forward around the notion of what Grossberg calls a "postmodern frontier." That is, they must put into place parameters that define when "America was what it should be" and when "America became what it is." This involves the historical designation of a period that marks the "fall of America."[20]

Like Thatcherism and Fascism, Bushism has constructed a glorious past that did not suffer from postmodern problems. The problems that did exist supposedly could be handled in a quick, effective manner that was agreeable to the majority of mythic America's populace. Pre-Bush the Son, the dividing line of this frontier was usually placed somewhere around the Vietnam years: the late sixties or early to midseventies. At that historical moment, the America of the fifties and sixties was seen as what the country should be, and the postsixties period was marked as the time of the "fall" into degeneration. Bushism now places the beginning of the postmodern frontier somewhere between 1992 and 2000 (the Clinton years) and marks September 11, 2001, as the actual frontier date when America's house of cards collapsed because of the Clinton administration's mismanagement.

Certainly, the America of the fifties and sixties was quite different from the one we know today. Some of these differences, however—especially the cultural ones—are not the reasons that America's "place" has changed on the global terrain. Bushism, however, engenders the belief that these are the precise changes that have led to the country's continuing demise. This is the realm that not only allows the existence of racism, classism, ethnic conflict, sexism, and other myopic divisions but also helps to create and cultivate them. Whether or not Bushites actually believe their rhetoric is really not the point. The point is that past-oriented discourse is an essential tool of domination, because it serves to actuate the next stage in the process: the creation of what Grossberg calls "affective (emotional) epidemics." These epidemics always function in a diversionary manner in that they emphasize false cleavages and crises that philosophies like Bushism can seize upon to influence public opinion.

For such a retrograde progression to take place, the people—of course—must cooperate. It must not be forgotten that cynicism and hopelessness are prerequisites for the numbing of the masses to occur. There must exist a general disinterest in alternate perspectives on the epidemics and a willingness to be lied to:

> The apparent success of such manipulation cannot be explained by falling back on images of the masses as intrinsically manipulatable, as cultural and ideological dopes. In fact, vast numbers know or assume that they are being lied to, or else they seem not to care. . . . This is precisely the paradox at the heart of contemporary U.S. politics and of the new conservatism's success. A large proportion of the population is outraged by at least some of what is going on, yet they remain inactive and uncommitted. There is a feeling of helplessness: what can anyone do?[21]

Eventually, the construction of the postmodern frontier and the use of affective epidemics leads to a mass of people who can be effectively moved in desired directions through the use of political deception, the media, or currently, the threat of terror. (Do what we say or the terrorists may get you next!) The people who have risen from the Bushist progression are now caught in a cycle of conceptual movement that is the psychological equivalent of "spaces without places."[22] They have forgotten where they belong, if they belong anywhere at all, and will therefore grab hold of the party line to fit in: wave their flags, sing "God Bless America," and support the "necessary" killing of Afghan, Iraqi, or Palestinian civilians while at the same time crying bloody murder when the same happens in New York or Washington, D.C.

The most troubling residual of September 11 and the rise of Bushism is, in fact, not the failure of black politicians such as Cynthia McKinney and Earl Hilliard to secure reelection; it is the loss of American political memory. To be sure, Bushist philosophy's ascent, and the defeat of these politicians are linked, but the attack on and reshaping of American institutional memory goes beyond these single issues. From local incidents to larger political realities, America's marginalized people are now faced with a chessboard that seems new but is in reality filled with old political players and recycled strategies from decades past. At the beginning of the twenty-first century, despite the reintroduction of political retreads such as Dick Cheney, the conservatives were winning many battles, because an environment had been constructed—at least in the short term—in which all was truly forgotten in the wake of the bombings and America's submersion into international bloodthirst.

As usual, when "larger issues" arose, concerns of black Americans were immediately forced into the shadows of the nation's (and some blacks') consciousness. In Cincinnati, for example, the police officer who killed young Timothy Thomas earlier in 2001 was released without punishment shortly after the September attacks. His exoneration was barely noted, even in the community that was moved to riot a few months earlier. In the face of the country's wallowing in the warm bath of New York police glorification, no one seemed to remember that this was the same police department whose officers had brutally shoved a plunger into Abner Louima's rectum. This was also the department that housed the officers who shot at the innocent Amadou Diallo forty-one times in front of his own home. They forgot that the newly knighted (by Britain, ironically) Rudolph Giuliani was the same man who had responded to the situations in a cold and callous way that many felt sent the message that Louima's and Diallo's suffering did not matter.

In the face of the flag waving and false unity, America continued to refuse to address its all-too-real, dirty little secrets—legacies of slavery, racism, and oppression that marginalized its black citizens to the point that many refused to join in the national self-congratulation. Many were righteously indignant that the core randomly labeled those who reminded them that America has not only wrought havoc throughout the world but has also caused incredible hurt, pain, and discontent at home, "unpatriotic troublemakers." American hard-line nationalists, conversely, argued that it was time for Americans to "come together" and dispense with compound American labels altogether. Ironically, their argument echoed the long-running French contestation that all French citizens were simply French—nothing else. This was one of the aspects of France many Americans adored, even though they hated the French's refusal to sign on to the Iraq War project. It was the cause of much anger in the States (remember "freedom fries"?).

Like most things, when the mask was peeled away, French Ward Conerlylike "deracialization" was not all it seemed. Largely because of its racial denial, in fall 2005 Paris was burning. It was the result of a reality that few Americans cared about and few of the French wanted to talk about. On its face, France had achieved what many Americans want: a raceless society. Legally, there are no black French citizens or white French citizens. They are all simply French. France is a self-proclaimed bastion of tolerance and social equality. In reality, it is anything but. While legal racial classification has been eradicated in

France, traditional racial recognition and discrimination are alive and well. On the outskirts of pristine and pampered Paris are working-class suburban ghettos (banlieues) populated by Arab and African immigrants, their children, and their grandchildren. They are reminders of France's own imperialism when it ventured into Algeria, Morocco, and other parts of the African world. Although their empire has crumbled, the human beings the French ripped from their cultures over a half-century ago remain.

The Africans' and Arabs' sojourn in the homeland of their former oppressors has not been easy. No laws exist to combat racial discrimination because race and racism, supposedly, do not exist in France. In reality, there is not a gap between theory and practice but a veritable chasm. Unemployment in France was an ongoing problem in late 2005. The overall rate had held steady around 10 percent for the last fifteen years. It was double that in the *banlieues* and approached 40 percent for nineteen to twenty-nine year olds whose parents were Moroccan or Algerian. Job applicants with traditional French names were also far more likely to be hired than those with Arab names. In the face of this suffering, when the *banlieues* exploded across the country and continent, French interior minister Nicolas Sarkozy proclaimed the "rioters" were "racaille" (scum, dregs, or gangrene, depending on one's translation). In other words, nothing is wrong with France; the problem lies with its ghetto dwellers. Riding the wave of this uberconservative message, the French elected Sarkozy president in May 2007.

Some have admitted that the *banlieues* were nothing more than tinderboxes created by racism, poverty, and indifference. If the French were willing to allow these segments of their population to languish in agony, they should not have been surprised when the uprisings came. Black and Arab children know their chances for success in France are slim to none. Many of them, in fact, want to come to America. They believe that even though America has continuing racial issues, it deals with them in word and deed. In effect, they want France to be more like America on issues of race. This is ironic indeed as many American blacks realized that while France's oppressed saw America as a model, Americans who were sick of race issues yearned to be more like France. September 11 was simply another reason to push discussions of race to the back burner once again.

As always, there were other black folk after September 11 quite anxious to "belong," who jumped on the "let's make war on the world" bandwagon. In separate Zogby and Gallup polls immediately following September 11, more than 70 percent of African Americans supported the racial profiling of Arabs. These same people apparently saw no cor-relation between this activity and the racial profiling American police departments had heaped upon blacks for years. Blacks were not alone. The transformation of the American mind in general was swift. Many citizens labeled George W. Bush "President Malaprop" a week before the bombings. A month after the attacks, he enjoyed an 84 percent approval rating (down from 91 percent two weeks earlier). Typical of the American public's turnaround was one woman exclaiming on national news, "These terrorists are dangerous and I'm afraid, but I know President Bush will take care of us." This was, to say the least, an interesting progression.

With regard to America's newly crowned law-enforcement and firefighting heroes, voices that reminded the country that many of America's fire and police departments (New York's included) have atrocious records where the hiring and promoting of minorities are con-cerned were muted. Besides this, the post–September 11 "United We Stand" front between New York's firefighters and police officers quickly proved disingenuous. Local New Yorkers are familiar with the long-standing bad blood between the city's police and firefighters, and the bombings did not completely dissipate it. Unfortunately, as most false unity does, their united front fell apart less than two months after it began when the city's firefighters clashed with police while protesting Giuliani's decision to scale back the number of rescue workers search-ing for bodies at the World Trade Center site. In the fracas, five police officers were injured and eleven firemen arrested, including the fire department's union leader. As with most events that did not fit into the idealized picture of post–September 11 America, the story was not widely publicized and was quickly forgotten.

Also disturbing, but not surprising, in a brazen display of capitalist greed, many people sought to turn nationalistic fervor into profit in the wake of September 11. There were television advertisements for "flag sets" that could be flown from one's car or home; videos commemorat-ing Pearl Harbor, which was often compared to the September 11 attacks; and a wide range of tee shirts, sweaters, sweatshirts, hats, and so on emblazoned with red, white, and blue or, in some extreme cases, hasty drawings of the twin towers themselves under attack. Someone even went so far as to offer a compact disc of patriotic songs. These endeavors proved once again that, in the midst of it all, one thing had not changed in America: money still mattered.

Barack Obama is lucky that he was not in the Senate when it voted whether or not to support America's foray into Iraq. However, he was in politics and proudly and accurately proclaims that he has always stood against the war. Surely, many others wish they could say the same. However, he will have to wrestle with the effects of September 11, Bushism (even after Bush leaves office), and the shifting ideology of black political leadership. This policy-making arm is one of the most important black leadership communities that merit our attention. As always, its ideological movements will seriously affect the fortunes of black America in particular and the country as a whole. Black political leadership is so crucial because it has a tradition of serving as part of the nation's political conscience. Who will speak to matters of conscience if black politicians lose theirs?

5

I Don't Care What Jesus Would Do; I've Got to Get Paid

The New Black Preacher

> Who says I am not under the special protection of God?
> —Adolf Hitler, after winning
> the 1933 German elections

In early summer 2006, Barack Obama took a step many of his Democratic colleagues had failed to take in recent years. Clearly lifting a page out of the Republican playbook, he rose to the podium of the National City Christian Church in Washington, D.C., and unapologetically linked religion and politics. At that point, columnist Jacob Weisberg labeled the speech the most important one Obama had delivered since his keynote at the Democratic Convention in 2004. Weisberg opined, "That earlier address, which set the political world spinning in Obama's direction, drew quietly on the religious imagery of 'things not seen.' This one confronted the problem of faith and politics directly."[1]

In one of his typical uberconservative rants, Alan Keyes flamed in 2004 that "Jesus Christ would not vote for Barack Obama." Obama ignored Keyes, proclaiming he was "running for senator, not minister."[2] Of course, he was able to flippantly dismiss Keyes' attacks, not just from the religious front but others as well, because Keyes was such a weak candidate. In the National City Christian Church speech, however, Obama took himself to task and labeled his approach a "typically liberal response" but said that the problem of religion had nagged at him:

75

[Obama stated that] in a country where "more people believe in angels than they do in evolution," Democrats would never be able to reach their fellow citizens so long as they continued to insist that religion and politics don't mix." In his remarks, Obama linked himself to literary and political figures who had God on their minds and in their voices. "If we scrub language of all religious content, we forfeit the imagery and terminology through which millions of Americans understand both their personal morality and social justice," he argued. "Frederick Douglass, Abraham Lincoln, William Jennings Bryan, Dorothy Day, Martin Luther King—the majority of great reformers in American history—were not only motivated by faith, but repeatedly used religious language to argue for their cause. So to say that men and women should not inject their 'personal morality' into public-policy debates is a practical absurdity."[3]

While all but refusing to link his eventual presidential campaign to issues of race and distancing himself from Jeremiah Wright (his sometimes-controversial Afrocentric Chicago pastor), Obama was no less than bold in his public wedding to mainstream American religious ideology. This played well in the main as well as with the oldest black leadership community: religious leaders.

Well before Obama's religious-political revelation in 2006, the presidential primaries and political wrangling of the contested general election of 2000 also helped illuminate the intersection between religion and politics that continues to concern a percentage of Americans. Certainly, many eyebrows were raised when Albert Gore Jr. selected conservative Democratic Connecticut Senator Joseph Lieberman, whom Barack Obama has called one of his mentors, as his running mate. Indisputably, the fact that Lieberman was the first Jewish American chosen to run atop a major national presidential ticket drew just as much attention as (or more attention than) his right-of-center politics.

On the Republican side of the house, many believe the religious Right had more than a little to do with the derailing of John McCain's candidacy for the Republican nomination. As the race between McCain and George W. Bush intensified, Pat Robertson, head of the Christian Coalition, showed his support for Bush by exclaiming, "If McCain wins the nomination, it will destroy the Republican Party."[4] Such attacks are common in politics, but the fact that Robertson is not a politician, but a man of God, led some to believe that his words carried special weight. Whether or not it was the influence of Robertson and his conservative religious compatriots, McCain's candidacy received heavy blows in Virginia—Robertson's home base. Two days before the presidential election, Bush again received a religio-political boost by being all but endorsed by the Reverend Billy Graham.

While Bush and McCain were the clear frontrunners for the Republican nomination and, according to Robertson and other religious rhetoricians, the affection of God, they were not alone. Before he began pestering Barack Obama four years later, Alan Keyes also ran for president in 2000 and pulled Republican primary discussions even farther to the moral and religious right with dogmatic statements such as the one in which he submitted America was suffering because "we have dethroned the authority of God."[5] While many people in mainstream America regard politicians and ministers such as Keyes and Robertson as dilettantes who have very little to contribute to balanced political discussion, others see them as moral compasses who should be heeded.

The African American community is also divided on the place of religious leaders and discourse in politics, but the lines between church and state are even more indistinct than in mainstream America. The black community has a long history of ministers doubling as political leaders. Because of their strong ties to religion and religious leaders, local and national black communities are especially susceptible to passively accepting sociopolitical stances submitted by men of God or those who invoke the name of God in their quasipolitical rhetoric. Such a reality, in many cases, leads to decisions that many who are politically informed see as retrograde:

> Beginning in the 1930s, a number of sociologists, including E. Franklin Frazier, have argued that the black church's "pie-in-the-sky," other-wordly orientation and its emotionalism work against the development of a black political consciousness and "this-world" concern with social change. Most recently, political scientist Adolph Reed, Jr. has asserted that the black church is at odds with the principles of democracy. He claims that despite the church's involvement in [Jesse] Jackson's presidential bids, church political activism is incompatible with modern, democratic political processes, given that the black church is intrinsically "nonpolitical," authoritarian, and conservative.[6]

These same critics deploy both Karl and Gary Marx to illustrate that, at times, religion can anesthetize rather than mobilize:

Critics of the black church base their arguments on the claim that religion is often depoliticizing, that is, "the opiate of the masses." Gary Marx's book, *Protest and Prejudice*, published in 1967, is frequently cited as empirical documentation of the antithetical relationship that exists between religion and politics for blacks. Marx found that religious blacks were less likely to be supportive of black civil rights militancy than non-religious blacks. The negative association between religiosity and militancy held even when other factors such as age, region, and social class, were taken into account.[7]

It is difficult to ignore the fact that whatever the black church's ideological orientation, it has hinged largely on black male ministerial leadership. While black men are generally marginalized in American society, it is clear that one zone of power they have secured in black America over time has been the pastorate. Even though black women continue to make inroads into this community of influence, the ministerial ranks are still dominated and viciously guarded by black males. Rupe Simms comments:

> In his recent work, [James] Cone confronts sexism in the African-American church. He boldly challenges male ascendance exhorting clergymen to assume responsibility for "the fullest development of [Black women's] potential for the service to God in the church and in society." He proposes "affirmative action for black women" in order to place them in "positions of responsibility" that "will reflect their percentage of the overall population."[8]

Womanist scholar Delores Williams powerfully confronts the church concerning its "multitude of sins against black women" that withholds from them "equal opportunity in . . . major leadership roles."[9] Williams specifically criticizes the all-too-often-encountered "sexual exploitation of black women" and the fact that "they are indoctrinated to be self-sacrificing and emotionally dependent on males."[10] Simms sums up Williams' arguments against the church:

> For Williams, [these realities] prevent women from reaching their full potential as individuals and as ministers serving their people through church-sponsored programs of community uplift and political liberation. Williams also criticizes the church for ministerial shortsightedness and self-absorption. To her the institution is unenlightened concerning the seriousness of the threat of the AIDS crisis and is blind

to the social destruction it creates by encouraging homophobia. In addition, she denounces the institution for "building and purchasing elaborate church edifices while thousands of black people live in dire poverty." She goes on to say that even these buildings are misused because they are "without viable programs to meet the needs of black women and the black community." Hence, for Williams, the church fails to actualize the full potential of its female constituency and its ability to serve the social and political needs of its community.[11]

Despite such protestations, little has changed in the black church as of yet. Even though black women continue to constitute the overwhelming majority of people sitting in the pews, male ministerial dominance and adherence to religious dogma is still so great in some instances that these same women are not allowed to even set foot in the churches' pulpits.

Obviously, one must exercise great care when addressing these issues. Painstaking sensitivity is necessary, because when the subject of the black church and its leaders is engaged the discussion is invariably colored by the fact that a good percentage of black Americans are cognitively influenced by their deep emotional ties to the sacred. The black community, maybe more than any other, is affectively linked to churches and their pastors to the degree that criticism of either (no matter how rational) is often viewed as nothing short of an attack on God. Such loyalty may be degenerative as well as generative in that it has opened the door equally wide for the entree of many of the race's greatest freedom fighters, as well as some of its most infamous demagogues. Unfortunately, black ministers (be they emancipators or collaborators in oppression) are often protected from secular intellectual confrontation by the almost certain ire of their flocks, which is heaped upon any critic who questions their leaders' decisions and/or motivations.

Few rational people would disagree with the assertion that many members of the black community are apt to follow ministers' leads on a wealth of issues that fall outside the province of religion proper. If the boundaries of black social and political ecology are indeed largely defined by the church, then it is only logical that the church be considered an important factor in black decision making when speaking not only to religious but also to sociopolitical realities and responses. While decisions limited to the day-to-day operation of their individual institutions may fall beyond the pail of intellectual contestation, when religious leaders' initiatives affect the political realities of local and national black communities, they must be taken to task in the realm of rational-critical discourse. This reality, combined with the fact that the political Right has displayed an affinity for programs and funding that center on "faith-based institutions," forces those committed to humanization to pursue rigorous, critical analyses of the direction of the black church even though such engagements all but ensure the consternation of many of the religiously devout.

The "Right" Partnerships: Black Religious Elites, Conservative Politicians, and Faith-Based Access Points

We would be wise to remember the words of Murray Stedman when he spoke to the price religious institutions may pay for political economic support in *Religion and Politics in America*:

> Freedom from economic control has been [more] difficult for the churches to achieve. Part of the difficulty is attributable to the concept that "he who pays the piper calls the tune," which may mean both that the payer does and ought to call the tune. We are told repeatedly, for example, that it would be immoral for the federal government to supply funds for public schools unless some measure of governmental control were instituted. The argument is that it is unethical and monetarily irresponsible to give money away without first attaching very tight strings, and, oppositely, that a church ought not to criticize people and institutions if it receives money from them.[12]

In the 1990s, many black churches' memberships grew to the point that they became what some observers dubbed "megachurches." While impressive numerically and positive socially in many respects, the arrival of the megachurch brought another residual that must be addressed. While business (fund-raising, institutional expansion, etc.) has always been an aspect of the black church, in many ways the black megachurch *is* a business. Unfortunately, along with the size, power, and influence such entities bring, they (like any other large business) also carry with them voracious appetites for economic resources that must be fed. Over time, the megachurch's projects extend it to the point that tithes and love offerings can no longer sustain it, and outside support must be sought. The reality of the link between economic support and limits on political criticism that Stedman illuminated is important once such an extension occurs.

Religious entities are certainly capable of offering constructive criticism to political players, and vice versa. In fact, there has actually been an elevation of public support for such involvement over the last three decades. In 1965, the Gallup Poll found that 53 percent of Americans believed that churches should not be involved in matters political, and 40 percent thought they should. Only 22 percent of those polled thought clergy should ever discuss political candidates or issues from the pulpit. Conversely, in 1996, 54 percent of those surveyed thought churches should be involved in politics. Of the people polled, 29 percent favored outright politicking from the pulpit.[13]

The increase in support for the wedding of religion and politics has mandated renewed discussion as to what role the church should play in the political process. While politics proper is solely concerned with the state apparatus of control that decides who gets what, when, where, and how, it is the religious community that ideally can offer moral guidance that may aid in humanizing this often brutal process. Historically, the place of religious institutions as moral critics has proven even more important in the African American community than in the main and religious arguments are at their best when they are able to stand outside the machinery of the state.

They lose their authenticity and the sincerity of their external place, however, when they enter the fray for money and power, which inherently drive the capitalist state. Stephen Carter believes religious involvement in politics is a double-edged sword: "The religious voice, at its best, is perhaps the only remaining force in politics that can call us to something more than our own selfish perspectives. . . . [But] a religious voice that becomes too settled in the secular political world, happily amassing influence and using it, is likely to lose its best and most spiritual self."[14]

Further complicating this dilemma, religious conservatism among black ministers is growing. Ideologically, many do not resemble reformers such as King or Fred Shuttlesworth at all. Pamela Howell provides several valuable vignettes of a few nationally known black megachurch ministers who have taken political stances clearly right of center. Of Kirbyjohn Caldwell, Howell writes:

> During the 2000 Republican National Convention, Houston-based preacher Kirbyjohn Caldwell introduced George W. Bush and was seen with Bush during his campaign. Though Caldwell declares himself an Independent, he says that he voted for Bush. Caldwell commented in a recent phone interview: "Traditionally, African Americans have

voted Democrat. We have voted for the party in spite of the person. It's now time that we vote for the person in spite of the party. We can't afford to vote blindly anymore. We have to vote on how a person's views line up with the word of God." Caldwell heads the 11,000-member Windsor Village United Methodist Church in Houston where he often teaches that success is attainable regardless of race or social background. He promotes Christian-based economic empowerment and has implemented many social and economic initiatives including a home-building program and a bank.[15]

On Atlanta-based televangelist and "prosperity preacher" Creflo Dollar, Howell opines:

> Though he has not publicly stated a party affiliation, Creflo Dollar, pastor of World Changers Church International in College Park, often praised Republican Alan Keyes during the early stages of the 2000 campaign. In December, he encouraged his congregation to support President-elect George W. Bush. Prior to that, Dollar had a private prayer meeting with Bush's attorney general appointee, John Ashcroft, who Dollar refers to as a personal friend. Dollar in a December 2000 sermon: "You're not a Democrat. You're not a Republican. You are a Christian, and you do not vote based on party. You vote based on the atmosphere that the person is going to create once they're in office. . . . If a guy gets in office and he creates an atmosphere to maintain somebody's sin, then I don't care if he is a Democrat. Democrat doesn't equal (pro) black." Dollar founded the 20,000-member World Changers Church International, which offers programs for employment, home-buying and other self-help guidance. Dollar has centered his message on financial prosperity and dependence on God rather than the government.[16]

Recently however, many black churches have indeed received financial help spearheaded by Republican politicians in the form of grants and other funding through faith-based initiatives. When religious figures and institutions form ties with politicians or political parties (which some have), criticisms of them must not be based in the realm of religion but on the policy-effects religious affiliations and loyalties bring. Without a doubt, there is a need for dialogue that is truly moral in tone. However, immoral policy should not be masked with supposedly moral supporters. Whenever it manifests itself, such a phenomenon must be challenged.

Herein lies the core problem plaguing new black church–Republican alliances formed in many places during George W. Bush's tenure in office. The key issue must always be retrograde national policy that cannot be ignored because politicians intermittently lead the charge for legislative grants for the largest black churches in various communities during election cycles. In effect, such financial support is tantamount to an attempt to buy nonquestioning black votes from members who proudly boast, "They helped our church." The greater question that should be asked is, "Do their national political policies help our people?"

It is essential that one is clear as to what constitutes the agenda the Republicans, their judicial appointees, and their allies espouse. These groups include, among others, a highly conservative, majority Republican appointed Supreme Court, Pat Robertson's Christian Coalition, the Center for Individual Rights, the Institute for Justice, the Federalist Society, the Center for Equal Opportunity, the American Civil Rights Institute, and the Southeastern Legal Foundation.

While the monikers of these organizations sound unimposing, they are at the heart of right-wing initiatives and court rulings such as the following: *Miller v. Johnson*, which declared the use of race as a dominant factor in drawing electoral district lines unlawful (this eradicated assurances that blacks would have national legislative representation in historically racist states); *Hopwood v. Texas*, which allowed an appeals court decision barring the University of Texas from considering race in admissions decisions to stand (this set the precedent for the eradication of affirmative action in Texas higher education); *Parents Involved in Community Schools v. Seattle School District No. 1*, which delivered a crushing blow to school desegregation plans based on race; and California's Civil Rights Initiative better known as Proposition 209, which destroyed affirmative action in California's public institutions.

These factions are also responsible for the advocacy of scathing cuts to higher education and healthcare; a much more vicious form of welfare reform than the one former president Bill Clinton signed into law; the erosion of hate speech and violence against women legislation; public-school privatization vouchers; anti-immigration and anti-immigrant's rights; antibilingual education and antibilingual usage; further assaults on affirmative action and public policy initiatives through the courts; and educational reforms that attack ethnic and gender studies that carve out space for minorities in the American academy. The list goes on and on. Taking these realities into account, most members of minority groups will answer "no" to the purely political question as to whether one should support a person who is a strong advocate of the Republican national agenda.

If these are the types of initiatives some black ministers now favor, they have a right to do so, but it is mandatory that those in their charge be very clear as to what they are supporting. When taken to task, the ideology that many of these men espouse sounds very close to what Cornel West has called "conservative behaviorism." West defines conservative behaviorists as ideologues who "promote self-help programs, black business expansion, and non-preferential job practices. They support vigorous free-market strategies that depend on fundamental changes in how black people act and live. To put it bluntly, their projects rest largely upon a cultural revival of the Protestant ethic in black America."[17] The lean of some ministers toward such an ideology is made clear in a number of passages such as the following, which displays unbalanced approaches to the relationship between behavior and structures that are common to behaviorist ideologues:

> I agree with the argument of those in the civil rights community who point out how social injustice and oppression have pernicious effects on the urban poor. However, I have also found merit in the position of men like Newt Gingrich, who draw a correlation between achievement and personal responsibility. I believe the old welfare system has often helped to foster illegitimate birth rates, joblessness and dependency because of the economic incentives to bear out-of-wedlock children and the disincentive to work. *While the African-American community continues to face the insidious evil of racism, I feel that at times we are often guilty of over-exaggerating our victimization and using it as an excuse for avoiding personal development.* (Emphasis added)[18]

Another minister intimates that he subscribes to such an ideology when proclaiming, "The black church has always seen a parallel between the children of Israel's captivity in Egypt and black people's captivity in America. . . . In this present hour, we are still fighting. There are still some things black people must do for themselves."[19] This minister continues by noting that these things include blacks improving their own economic and social consciousness instead of asking for assistance from government leaders and the white community. This was an ironic stance for one who had received hefty amounts of governmental assistance from his city's Democrat-dominated Board of Aldermen as well as a federal grant sponsored by a Republican congresswoman.

Some believe the self-help position is shored up by statements such as "the bottom stratum of the black community has compelling problems that can no longer be blamed solely on white racism. These problems will not yield to protest marches or court orders."[20] Even though some conservative ministers concede that the protest tactics of civil rights activists will always be needed to combat institutional racism, they often reaffirm their belief in behaviorist-centered ideological models by countering, that "there is also a need for faith-based, grass-roots, self-help approaches which help youth deal with behavioral problems, community values, academic remediation, attitudes and beliefs about responsibility, work, family, education and goal setting."[21]

Howell's evaluation of the current political stances of prominent black minister (and former Democratic congressional representative) Floyd Flake further illustrates that the self-help paradigm is alive and well in today's black church:

> While George W. Bush campaigned in New York last year, Rev. Floyd Flake, pastor of the Allen African Methodist Episcopalian Church in Queens, escorted him. Flake says the appearance with Bush was not an endorsement, and he has refused to be pigeonholed politically. A registered Democrat, Flake broke party ranks when it came to abortion and gay rights and frequently forged bipartisan alliances on economic issues. In an interview last year, Flake commented: "Black preachers have become an appendage in the Democratic Party. That's why I'm apolitical now. I want both parties to deal with me." Flake, who served in the U.S. Congress for 11 years, often cites his own example of what can be done through hard work and Christian values. He has created a senior center, credit union and school and has always preached the importance of self-motivation. Flake resigned from Congress in November 1997 to focus on his 12,000-member church, which he says is an excellent example of the "Bible-and-bootstrap ethic."[22]

While many religious and political conservatives now use the words of King to support paradigms emphasizing self-help-based philosophies, King himself warned:

> Now there is another myth that still gets around: It is a kind of over-reliance on the bootstrap philosophy. There are those who still feel that if the Negro is to rise out of poverty, if the Negro is to rise out of the slum conditions, if he is to rise out of discrimination and

> segregation, he must do it all by himself. And so they say the Negro
> must lift himself by his own bootstraps. . . . They never stop to real-
> ize that no other ethnic group has been a slave on American soil.
> The people who say this never stop to realize that the nation made
> a black man's color a stigma. But beyond this they never stop to
> realize the debt that they owe a people who were kept in slavery two
> hundred and forty-four years. . . . It's all right to tell a man to lift
> himself by his own bootstraps, but it is a cruel jest to say to a boot-
> less man that he ought to lift himself by his own bootstraps.[23]

There are a number of philosophical points of contention raised by conservative engagements. The most obvious is that they present false ideological choices where behavior and hegemonic institutions are concerned. There is a dichotomization of institutional realities to which marginalized citizens are subjected and the life chances and behavior that result from them. While many ministers now dismiss civil rights activities in the tradition of King such as protest marches and attacks on local, state, and federal judicial entities as outdated (which is true to some extent), they never note that there is an inextricable link between challenges to the state (maybe in different, more progres-sive forms), eventual institutional change, and black personal and col-lective humanization. Such stances are common to conservative behaviorists, but after the rhetoric is dismantled it becomes clear that they place an inordinate amount of blame for dysfunctionality and suf-fering on oppressed people rather than oppressive structures.

As King did, we must continuously guard against religious emo-tionalism clouding our judgment on matters political. The black com-munity must learn to deal with the quandaries religious affiliation may present. Clearly, even when ministers vote for conservatives (as Kir-byjohn Caldwell admitted he did for George W. Bush), their individual support cannot be classified as immoral, wrong, or destructive. In and of itself, their individual support is of little consequence. What is of consequence, however, is the effect this support or even the perception of it has on the flocks they lead. The fact that a percentage of church members follow what they perceive to be their pastors' example and support conservative candidates who, otherwise, would never be con-sidered viable politicians for blacks to embrace once again illustrates the inordinate influence ministers wield in the black community.

To be fair, the power these reverends enjoy is not new, nor did they single-handedly create it. The black preacher has always had a dispro-portionate amount of power and influence in the black community.

This has held true from Henry McNeil Turner to Martin Luther King Jr. to Jesse Jackson. Rarely do followers question such men about their stances or actions. They are usually embraced as the chosen ones of God, and this places them in unique positions of authority in the highly religious black community. While this faith in men of the cloth has always been potentially dangerous, very few black ministers have supported politicians or political agendas that marginalize the majority of blacks on the national level.

Maybe Martin Delany, the father of black nationalism, was correct in 1852 when he said, "The colored races are highly susceptible of religion; it is a constituent principle of their nature, and an excellent trait in their character. But unfortunately for them, they carry it too far."[24] An argument certainly can be made that many black men are fine ministers in the black Christian tradition who deliver emotive, religious messages from the pulpit on Sunday mornings. But when they cross into the realm of politics, they need to be taken to task with rational-critical discourse free of religious emotion. Black people would be well served by strongly challenging these men on their real or perceived support of politicians who openly advocate political agendas based on xenophobic cleavages.

Though often ignored or misunderstood, inquiries such as this must ultimately be concerned with the intersection of epistemological engagement and axiological shifts in black culture. Often there is the attempt to separate religious stances and these matters of the mind into distinct, disconnected entities. The reality, however, is that if one interrogates a religious populace's epistemic modes of inquiry while disregarding its conclusions concerning values and ethics, a critical link that can help explain political behavior is lost. It must be clear that epistemology is not simply the authority by which one purports to base his or her knowledge. Certainly, the questions "What do I know?" and "How do I know it?" are asked in epistemological inquiry, but the real power of the engagement does not end there. Once people draw conclusions about what they know and how they know it (whether the answers are right or wrong), they use this knowledge to construct, affirm, and reaffirm individual and group modes of behavior and traditions. These behaviors and traditions are ultimately based on, and subsequently help to create, ethical constructs.

Troubling questions rise out of this progression. What if the answers to the initial epistemic questions are wrong? What if an individual draws conclusions and inferences from skewed, flawed, or even outright false political information? Beyond this, there exists the possibility that the formation of identities, political stances, and the axiological foundations upon which they necessarily rest could be exposed to a dangerous domino effect. Such an effect occurs if inquiries and answers concerning the authoritative legitimacy of knowledge is not grounded in fact but fiction. Carried far enough and reified long enough, not only do the answers to questions become wrong, but the questions themselves become flawed. From these flaws, political decision making stands a greater probability of colonization and exploitation. If epistemological inquiry is necessarily related to the construction of ethical systems, then it may very well be mandatory that our study of the subject at hand be rooted in epistemological means with the purpose of influencing axio-logical and political ends.

Without a doubt, epistemological exploitation is aided if the oppressed dedicate themselves to religious structures and leaders with such fervor that space for dialectical challenge is crushed. The human-ization of black America suffers if contestations to ideologies and move-ments that would, in the main, be considered politically retrograde can protect themselves from criticism through the use of religious loyalty and the all-too-often-unquestioned panacea of faith. While the fact that the black church and its leaders have sat at the heart of the black humaniza-tion project for many years cannot be denied, we must be forever vigilant that they never mutate into tools used to contribute to black suffering. Whether degenerative contributions are intentional or not does not mat-ter if the results derail the ongoing struggle to carve out social and polit-ical space into which the black collective can enter with dignity.

Earlier, George W. Bush's faith-based initiative was cited as a new political reality that forces those concerned with the continuing black freedom struggle to examine the new intersection between conserva-tive American politics and the black church. Bush's promotion of ties to religious institutions raised constitutional concerns from the Left as well as the Right. For the black community, troubling issues run deeper than the possibility of constitutional circumvention. In reality, govern-mental links to the religious community did not begin with Bush. In fact, Clinton's welfare reform bill had a faith-based component built into it. Bush's initiative, however, is of special concern because it is overblown and appeals to the religious right with possibly insidious consequences for the African American community. Bush's approach is nothing more than a variation on a strategic theme that cultivates direct ties to black communities through religious channels while simultaneously deleting more politically astute blacks (politicians, intellectuals, etc.) from the political equation.

True to the strategies of the Right, the faith-based initiative heralds the coming of yet another machination that overlooks structural American sociopolitical flaws in an effort to take governmental responsibility for the condition of the historically disenfranchised away from government. In this particular case, the black church's place in the political lives of black people is inflated to a dangerous magnitude from which its largely conservative ideologies can be reinforced in the main. Beyond this fact, the faith-based paradigm creates a situation in which large amounts of government dollars targeted to the religious community fall into the hands of a small number of elite black ministers who seem increasingly preoccupied with an extraordinary ethic of capitalist consumption.

The money gained by most (not all) of these men rarely filters down to the suffering masses. There is no reason to believe the faith-based initiative will change this reality. While the black collective, more than likely, will not be aided, such partnerships between members of the black religious aristocracy and the conservative political Right does help establish a political anchor in black communities through the defacto purchase of the votes of a percentage of these religious leaders' followers. With the rise of the black megachurch, a small number of individual ministers and the 501c3 nonprofit arms of their ministries are garnering unprecedented profits, but they do little that really helps solve the social, political, and cultural problems that continue to marginalize many in the black community. Ultimately, many of these organizations conservatively assign moral value to people's behavior without engaging the structural inequities of American society which target, criminalize, and dehumanize black people. Black progress has always been a result of faith, individual responsibility, *and* systemic struggle and resistance. Black religious conservatives have begun to ignore the efficacy of the last component.

Bible and Bling: Confronting the New Black Church

The unfortunate history of America's relationship to its darker hued sons and daughters has taught us that black human dignity must be fought for and continuously protected once achieved. It would be wise to remember that most black progress has not been the result of white crises of conscience or the praxis of European-descended saviors who have rescued the race from its drudgery. Contrarily, it has been African Americans who have served in the vanguard of liberatory struggle by speaking to the true ideals of the land. Du Bois commented in *The Gift of Black Folk:*

Dramatically the Negro is the central thread of American history. The whole story turns on him whether we think of the dark and flying slave ship in the sixteenth century, the expanding plantations of the seventeenth, the swelling commerce of the eighteenth, or the fight for freedom of the nineteenth. It was the black man who raised a vision of democracy in America such as neither Americans nor Europeans conceived in the eighteenth century and such as they have not even accepted in the twentieth; and yet a conception which every clear sighted man knows is true and inevitable.[25]

Du Bois goes on:

The great vision of the black man was, of course, at first the vision of the few, as visions always are, but it was always there; it grew continuously and it developed quickly from wish to active determination. . . . The democracy established in America in the eighteenth century was not, and was not designed to be a democracy of the masses of men and it was thus singularly easy for people to fail to see the incongruity of democracy and slavery. It was the Negro himself who forced the consideration of this incongruity, who made emancipation inevitable and made the modern world at least consider if not wholly accept the idea of a democracy including men of all races and colors.[26]

The significant role of blacks in the formation of the American republic and their own emancipation forces us to be leery of approaches, religious or otherwise, that take agency out of the hands of the black collective and entrusts its well-being to the whims of others. The obvious question here is, Why would such paths be taken by any members of the African American community? If salient, such undertakings will almost always be condemned as wrong-headed at best and malevolent at worst. Problems arise, however, when politically regressive agendas are shrouded by the establishment of religiopolitical partnerships. In the final analysis, we are duty bound to take strong stands and root these problems out when they rear their heads. If we are to move forward and truly maintain, rediscover, and reaffirm revolutionary critical consciousness, we must not be paralyzed by fear and silenced by trepidation when we are threatened by issues such as these—even when they come from within.

Undoubtedly, some people have taken notice. While *Black Enterprise* ran a cover story praising megachurch ministers Eddie Long,

T. D. Jakes, and Kirbyjohn Caldwell, University of Illinois professor John Fountain expressed increasing concern about the black church's direction. In late summer 2005, Fountain raised eyebrows when he published an article in the *Washington Post* explaining why he no longer attends church. At times, Fountain's commentary was nothing short of scathing:

> [The black church] seems to have turned inward. It seems to exist for the perpetuation of itself—for the erecting of grandiose temples of brick and mortar and for the care of pastors and the salaried administrative staff. Not long ago, a preacher friend confided: "The black church is in a struggle for its collective soul—to find itself in an age when it is consumed by the God of materialism." This preoccupation with the material world is pervasive, and has bred a culture that has left a trail of blood and tears in black neighborhoods across the country with little collective outcry from the church. Still, it's one thing for the world to be ensnared by the trappings of materialism— but the church?
>
> I am incensed by Mercedes-buying preachers who live in suburban meadows far from the inner-city ghettos they pastor, where they bid parishioners to sacrifice in the name of God. I am angered by the preacher I know, and his wife and co-pastor, who exacted a per diem and drove luxury vehicles, their modest salaries boosted by tithes and offerings from poor folks in a struggling congregation of families, a number of them headed by single women. This at a time when the church didn't own a single chair and was renting a building to hold worship services.

Fountain continues:

> I have come to see the countless annual meetings and church assemblies, camouflaged as worship services, as little more than fundraisers and quasi-fashion shows with a dose of spirituality. I am disheartened by the territorialism of churches, vying for control and membership, as a deacon at a Baptist church said to me recently, in much the same way as gangs, rather than seeing themselves as communal partners in a vineyard with one Lord and a single purpose.
>
> But even in an age of preacher as celebrity, it is not the evolution of a Bling Bling Gospel that most disheartens me. It is the loss of the church's heart and soul: the mission to seek and to save lost souls

through the power of the Gospel and a risen savior. As the homicide toll in black neighborhoods has swelled, I've wondered why churches or pastors have seldom taken a stand or ventured beyond the doors of their sanctuaries to bring healing and hope to the community— whether to stem the tide of violence and drugs, or to help cure poverty and homelessness or any number of issues that envelop ailing black communities.[27]

Obviously, Fountain's stand sparked hearty, though short-lived, discussion in many black communities. It should be noted that Fountain is not your typical critic of today's new breed of prosperity-preaching ministers or churches. The former *Washington Post* journalist is actually a licensed minister himself who, like me, grew up in a Pentecostal church. He is no atheist, outsider, or professional troublemaker. It seems he was just fed up. The response to Fountain from many in the black religious community was typical. Many said they understood his concerns, but he did the wrong thing by leaving the church: he should have stayed and tried to change it from within. Obviously, they totally missed his explanation about what happens to people who speak up:

> Further contributing to my disappearing act is that, after being put down and put upon in a society that relegates black men largely to second-class status, the last place I want to feel that way is at church. And yet, in the church, where I have at times in my life felt the most uplifted, I have at other times felt greatly diminished, most often by insecure leaders. If such leaders feel threatened by your ability to speak or preach or teach better than they, or by the fact that you think differently from them, or by the fact that you possess some other social badge they do not—like a college education—then they perceive you as stealing a little of their sheen in the public's eyes. And you become subject to the same kind of shunning and subtle disconnection that I have seen and known in the professional world.[28]

Others thought Fountain should be dismissed altogether. One local minister, while basking in a bath of smugness and arrogance, stated at a meeting I attended that writings such as Fountain's really did not matter because "the victory of the church has already been won." Translation: "We can do whatever we want, and no criticism changes that." Despite this minister's hubris, Fountain is not alone. Nobody in black America can claim ignorance anymore about what is going on in many houses of praise. Like Fountain, many blacks have left the church. Others, of course, have committed themselves to staying—no matter what. Regardless of which group we belong to now, black people must own who and what many of our churches and religious leaders have become. We must own the incredible debauchery heaped upon black people in cities across the country. We must own our support of exploitative political partnerships, ministerial arrogance, congregational narrow-mindedness, mean-spiritedness, hostility, and at times, outright greed. We must own it all. As Obama finds his spiritual voice, let us hope he finds a critical one as well.

6

Before and Beyond Don Imus

On BET, Hip-Hop Culture, and Their Consequences

Rap music stated its position [in the 1980s], thoroughly evaluating many American icons, although in the process seemed to lose itself by connecting to the corporate umbilical cord.

—Chuck D, from the foreword to Dive Zirin,
Welcome to the Terrordome: The Pain,
Politics, and Promise of Sports

I am absolutely convinced that, internal to the race, BET has done more damage to black people than any other single entity in the last 40 years.

—Mawuli Mel Davis, Atlanta Attorney
and Community Activist (2007)

The belief that Barack Obama had the capacity to connect with America's youth was often voiced during the early days of his 2008 presidential run. As we have seen, Obama definitely has a particular flair that appeals to constituencies across many lines, including generational ones. Conversations that utilize the broad-stroked term *youth* in twenty-first-century America, however, invite the question, Which youths are we really talking about? No conversation about young people is relevant in black America unless we include the group we have quite appropriately, though in some respects disturbingly, labeled the "hip-hop generation."

95

This group of teens and twenty-somethings, submerged within both generations X and Y, is largely defined by elevating their wedding of the most popular music of their time with culture to unusual levels. Certainly, jazz, rock and roll, folk, rhythm and blues, soul and other musical forms impacted American and global culture. That said, none has defined an entire generation of Americans to the degree hip-hop has. So, the larger question may not be if Obama can appeal to youth, but can he specifically appeal to American youth impacted by hip-hop?

In the late seventies, many witnessed the genesis and promulgation of rap music's early forms. Widely considered a musical fad at the time, there was no way to know that the catchy tunes of the Sugar Hill Gang, Curtis Blow, and others would have staying power. In fact, early rappers introduced artistic and entertainment variations that, over the next quarter century, would morph into what we now know as hip-hop and become the world's largest selling recorded medium. Beyond that, and maybe more important, many (especially youth and those interested in accessing youth constituencies) now actually regard hip-hop artists and moguls as a new and extremely influential black leadership community. The impact of these realities on many aspects of American culture in general, and black culture in particular cannot be overstated.

Being a member of generation X, the influences of rap and hip-hop were unavoidable in my life. I was an elementary school student when the Sugar Hill Gang released "Rapper's Delight." Like every youngster at the time, I knew every word (or, as adulthood and karaoke machines have proven to so many of us, at least I thought I did). I remember when there was no debating who the best rappers were in the early 1980s. It was Run DMC. Run, "D," and "J" (the late Jam Master J) were the best, and everyone else was a distant second. I remember when LL Cool J was just a skinny teenager belting out the lyrics of "Radio" with unparalleled force. I remember when Luke Skywalker (later just "Luke" and then "Uncle Luke" after a pesky George Lucas lawsuit) and the 2 Live Crew changed everything in the mideighties with their uninhibited sexual content. I remember when the violent lyrics of NWA (Niggaz with Attitudes) shocked the nation a few years later.

As I made my way through college, my friends and I found Malcolm X, the Black Panthers, SNCC, and the movements that bred them. We read nonstop and rooted our ideas of manhood and decency in these heroes of the 1960s. Rap was still there. Acronym monikers for our favorite groups ran rampant, and their music is unforgettable. PE (Public Enemy), BDP (Boogie Down Productions), PRT (Poor Righteous Teachers), X-Clan (well, they were just X-Clan), and a host of other artists provided the theme music for my young adulthood. Many of them were what people now call "political or conscious rappers." In the late eighties and early nineties when I was completing college, we did not call them that: we just called them "rappers." Times change. In fact, what was then considered the most gutter form of hip-hop (gangsta rap—before it was even called "gangsta rap") is now mainstream, and conscious rap is "underground."

No matter one's opinion of hip-hop, it is currently king. Not jazz, blues, R&B, soul, funk, country, folk or classical—hip-hop dominates. Modifications to certain genres (the gangsta rap variant in particular) seem to be the single greatest contribution of an entire generation of black youth to the world. While hip-hop, at its best, has endless potential as a positive politicizing force, many of its realities force us to ask the serious question: As it stands, is hip-hop really helping or hurting?

The distinction between rap and hip-hop may seem trivial (and is overlooked by many), but placing them in one monolithic category is problematic. In fact, the cleavages distinguishing rap and hip-hop are profoundly important to many of today's youth. In the 1980s, then-budding hip-hop mogul Russell Simmons directed his employees not to sell rap/hip-hop as music but as a culture. Even a cursory look at Simmons' empire—from Def Jam Music, to his partnership with HBO to offer the *Def Comedy Jam* and *Def Poetry* television shows, to his immensely lucrative Phat Farm clothing line—proves his strategy was successful.

In most current youth culture circles, rap is regarded merely as music, and hip-hop is hailed as a way of life carrying its own dress, rhetoric, rules, perspectives on the world, and measurements of achievement. In many ways, Simmons was a visionary. Hip-hop most certainly is now regarded by many as a culture—so much so that an entire generation is identified by the hip-hop brand. Reinforcement of hip-hop as culture is widespread and ongoing. For instance, longtime MC and hip-hop spokesman KRS-One founded an organization called the "Temple of Hip-Hop" which promotes hip-hop as a culture. To be fair, KRS-One, former frontman of Boogie Down Productions, is widely considered highly politicized and "positive." Problematically, the KRS-Ones of hip-hop are not currently among its most influential personalities. For every KRS-One, there are five Lil' Waynes. For every Talib Kweli, there are ten 50 Cents. For every Chuck D, there are twenty Young Jeezys. Gangsta rap rules the landscape, and few people—other than those unquestioningly wedded to its culture—argue that gangsta rappers are defined by a wealth of redeeming characteristics. Without a doubt, like it or not, gangsta rappers rule the roost, and youth dedication to them is almost religious.

Analysis of the role of hip-hop and its colossal impact on both black and American public spheres raises a host of issues. However disturbing it may be, we must begin to seriously engage the general departure of many of hip-hop's tributary genres from any commitment to the construction of mediated spaces and cultural norms that reinforce, rather than annihilate, progressive oppositional socialization and movements. Considering this social and political fact, three major issues emerge. First of all, historical, sociological, and political conceptualizations of the public sphere as an equally accessible communal realm of political and civil society where public opinion is formed through the use of rational-critical discourse are logical starting points when speaking to the construction of black mediated spaces that produce, reflect, or reinforce progressive black culture. Next, hip-hop culture's reification of what many would argue are often retrograde ethics introduces perspectives on morality and collective politicization that hamstring the construction of media forms and black identities that effectively speak to issues of social, political, and psychological repression.

Finally, in response to this reality the black Left must continuously seek to construct oppositional mediated spaces whose aims are not necessarily to destroy hip-hop but certainly to expose exploitive structures and doctrines within the art/entertainment form. We must face this charge squarely and create space for honest and constructive sociopolitical discourse on the very real fallout of the conflation and normalization of hip-hop culture *as* black culture. At this point, in many quarters this has not been done without the questioning of critics' racial authenticity, ideological, and political orientation.

Patterson and Cosby: Concerns before Imus

In April 2007, America's racial divide was again illuminated when radio "shock jock" Don Imus referred to members of Rutgers University's predominantly black women's basketball team as "nappy-headed hos." Imus's comments set off a firestorm of criticism from some circles and eventually led to the termination of the simulcast of his show by MSNBC as well as his release from CBS Radio. One side of the argument was that Imus' words smacked of racial insensitivity and sexism. Reinforcing this stance was the fact that Imus has a history of such transgressions. This one simply got the most press.

Indeed, Imus's list of offenses was long. He referred to respected black journalist, author, and sports critic William Rhoden as a "quota hire." According to a Mike Wallace report on *60 Minutes*, Imus said he picked a particular producer to do "nigger jokes" on air.[1] He called political analyst and television personality Gwen Iffil a "cleaning lady" and had referred to other blacks as "monkeys" and "knuckle draggers." In fact, John Leo commented that these references went so far that in 2001, black journalist and commentator Clarence Page wrestled a public pledge from Imus that he would "cease all simian references to black athletes" and ban "all references to non-criminal blacks as thugs, pimps, muggers and Colt 45 drinkers."[2] Disturbingly, outside of Page's challenge, Imus seemingly functioned with impunity for years:

> Mr. Page is a rare example of a well-known journalist challenging the inflammatory rhetoric [of Imus]. Imus's prominent guests almost never get around to criticizing his vitriol. Fairness and Accuracy in Reporting (FAIR), a left-of-center press watchdog group, points out that in 2000 Tim Russert suggested that George W. Bush's appearance at Bob Jones University was "giving affirmation to that institution." Mr. Russert asked Mr. Bush, "Why are you associating with them?" Obviously, the same question can be asked about Mr. Russert's cozy relationship with Imus. *New York Times* eminence Frank Rich, a regular Imus guest, is ever alert to smears of gays and women and virtually went into a swoon when George Allen used the word "macaca." Yet a computer search failed to turn up any complaints from Mr. Rich about Imus's bigoted remarks.

> During Imus's abusive speech at the radio and TV correspondents' dinner in 1998, there was talk of walking out on the speaker. It didn't happen. Later there was murmuring of a celeb boycott but the only notable to declare one was Cokie Roberts. ("I really don't think it would be appropriate for any of us to go back on.") Imus abused her on air, and Ms. Roberts returned.[3]

Others sympathized with Imus and regarded his plight the product of black hypocrisy and hypersensitivity. This camp saw fit to simply ignore (or did not know about) Imus' track record of racially offensive speech. They framed his comments as lighthearted with nonoffensive, humorous intent. In their opinion, Imus—not the Rutgers basketball team in particular or black people in general—was the victim at the end of the day. Foundational to their argument was the belief that black America was submerged in a culture that normalized, and even embraced, language far worse than Imus's. So why crucify Imus for something that went on in black America every day without incident? As a result, condemnations of hip-hop culture took center stage in attempts to defend Imus. For good or ill, by late 2007 Imus was back on the air. What many people ignored (or again did not know) was the fact that a spirited and ongoing conversation about hip-hop was already alive and kicking in black America.

Beginning in March 2006, Harvard sociologist Orlando Patterson's opinion editorial "A Poverty of the Mind" appeared in newspapers throughout the country and became the latest in a long line of critiques of hip-hop and its consequences. Patterson wasted no time laying down the gauntlet with a controversial indictment of recent social science approaches to the study of the many plights of America's black youths:

> Several recent studies have garnered wide attention for reconfirming the tragic disconnection of millions of black youths from the American mainstream. But they also highlighted another crisis: the failure of social scientists to adequately explain the problem, and their inability to come up with any effective strategy to deal with it. The main cause for this shortcoming is a deep-seated dogma that has prevailed in social science and policy circles since the mid-1960's: the rejection of any explanation that invokes a group's cultural attributes—its distinctive attitudes, values and predispositions, and the resulting behavior of its members—and the relentless preference for relying on structural factors like low incomes, joblessness, poor schools and bad housing.[4]

Maybe the most contentious part of "A Poverty of the Mind" is delivered toward its conclusion when Patterson addresses the question of why young black men are dropping out of high school at record numbers. He places a good deal of blame squarely at the feet of hip-hop culture:

> Their [black males'] candid answer [to why they were "flunking out"] was that what sociologists call the "cool-pose culture" of young black men was simply too gratifying to give up. For these young men, it was almost like a drug, hanging out on the street after school, shopping and dressing sharply, sexual conquests, party drugs, Hip-Hop music and culture, the fact that almost all the superstar athletes and a great many of the nation's best entertainers were black. Not only was living this subculture immensely fulfilling, the boys said, it also brought them a great deal of respect from white youths. This also explains the

otherwise puzzling finding by social psychologists that young black men and women tend to have the highest levels of self-esteem of all ethnic groups, and that their self-image is independent of how badly they were doing in school.

I call this the Dionysian trap for young black men. The important thing to note about the subculture that ensnares them is that it is not disconnected from the mainstream culture. To the contrary, it has powerful support from some of America's largest corporations. Hip-Hop, professional basketball and homeboy fashions are as American as cherry pie. Young white Americans are very much into these things, but selectively; they know when it is time to turn off 50 Cent and get out the SAT prep book. For young black men, however, that culture is all there is—or so they think. Sadly, their complete engagement in this part of the American cultural mainstream, which they created and which feeds their pride and self-respect, is a major factor in their disconnection from the socioeconomic mainstream.[5]

Not surprisingly, Patterson drew both applause and criticism from across the ideological spectrum. Some hailed his missive as a needed engagement that called for black folk to look in the mirror at their own behavior for encouraging the ongoing plight of young black males. Others saw it as another in a long line of articles written by black intellectuals who, at worst, hated themselves and wished to take it out on the rest of black folk or, at best, were disconnected from the life worlds of the masses. I certainly believe Patterson's approach has a few problems. Most glaringly, while it may not be his intention (and I do not believe it is), a reader may leave "A Poverty of the Mind" with the belief that individual behavior and structures can be neatly bifurcated. Contrarily, the individual effort/behavior concentration of most conservatives and the structural preoccupation of many liberals indeed has a synthesis. Structures and behavior are inextricably linked—consistently creating, supporting, and reifying one another without end. Patterson alludes to this fact, but he does not take the analysis far enough.

Patterson also is a bit careless at times in an effort to support his stance that culture/behavior hold more explanatory power than structural engagement. The clearest example of this is his view of Jim Crow and its fall. He asserts that Jim Crow was a "deeply entrenched set of cultural and institutional practices built up over four centuries of racist domination and exclusion of blacks by whites in the South." While admitting that Jim Crow was "institutional," Patterson then wheels in the next sentence and states, "Nothing could have been more cultural than that." He then lightens Jim Crow's significance by claiming America was able to "dismantle the entire system within a single generation, so much so that today blacks are now making a historic migratory shift back to the South, which they find more congenial than the North."[6]

Patterson's relegating of the effects of Jim Crow to "a single generation" is certainly arguable, but his notion that it was the epitome of an almost strictly cultural phenomenon is misleading. Without a doubt, Jim Crow had undeniable cultural elements, but it also had powerful political and economic underpinnings that should not be discounted in such a cavalier manner. Even with these critiques in mind, Patterson should probably not be dismissed as a self-loathing uberconservative plagued with the paradigmatic myopia that usually accompanies such ideology. While clearly not currently a leftist, it would also be incorrect to place him in the camps of Shelby Steele or John McWhorter. In fact, the Jamaican-born Patterson has been known to take America to task in oral and written word for some time.

In spite of Patterson's belief that social scientists have largely "[rejected] any explanation that invokes a group's cultural attributes," critiques of black behavior and cultural norms are not novel. To be sure, Patterson's criticism is not the most famous in recent years (though it is arguably better thought out). That honor lies outside intellectual circles with actor/comedian and *Come On, People* author Bill Cosby. During a celebration of the fifty-year anniversary of the landmark *Brown v. Board of Education* decision in 2004, Cosby caused a stir in the African American community when he accused a good percentage of the black dispossessed of not holding up "their end of the bargain." While whites generally remained silent or neutral, Cosby's comments mobilized both criticism and praise from many quarters of the black community. University of Pennsylvania professor and leading public intellectual Michael Eric Dyson, who has been embraced by black youth culture more than most of his contemporaries in academe, immediately called Cosby into question by characterizing his comments as "classist, elitist and rooted in generational warfare."[7]

Spelman College professor and *To the Break of Dawn: A Freestyle on the Hip-Hop Aesthetic* author William Jelani Cobb's critique of "America's favorite dad" contextualized Cosby's stance as nothing new. Cobb opined that the comedian's lambasting of poorer blacks was a continuation of the long-running disdain among the black bourgeoisie of their "less fortunate cousins":

"Respectable" blacks have long felt it necessary to clean up, dust off and lead their less fortunate cousins into the promised land of social acceptance. When it all gets down to the get-down, black people are no more immune to believing stereotypes about African Americans than anyone else—and Cosby's podium-pounding was full of the grossest stereotypes of poor black people. Even if you agreed with his hyperbolic claims of $500 sneakers taking precedence over Hooked on Phonics in the hood, even if you signed on to his 21st century bootstrap prescriptions ("You can't blame white people for this"), it's impossible to ignore the classist, bigoted and reactionary underpinnings of his disdain for giving black children names like Shaniqua or Ali, or his justification of police shooting people in the back of the head for "stealing pound cake." (I have to wonder what Cosby would say to me, a black man with a Ph.D. and no criminal record, who has, nonetheless, had police pull guns on him three times in his life—once by an officer demanding that I walk on the sidewalk and not the street). In the wake of Amadou Diallo and Abner Louima, in the wake of literally dozens of black people being arrested and imprisoned on false evidence in Tulia, Texas two years ago these comments are not only ignorant, but extremely dangerous.[8]

While there was no shortage of disapproval from the black Left, Cosby was certainly not without his supporters. Many blacks rushed to his defense and fervently argued the point that black folk had to begin taking responsibility for their own condition and fate. They saw Cosby's denouncement of degenerative popular culture as painful but necessary and cogent. According to them, black adults and youth were largely victims of their own debauchery—disinterest in education, gutter language and speech patterns, overfascination with the worst of hip-hop culture, romanticization of "thug life" and gangsterism, and an aversion to work.

Ironically, after taking the black masses to task for poor familial skills and dedication, Cosby (who had already admitted to an extended extramarital affair years earlier) took another personal hit in early 2005 when he was accused of inappropriately touching two females in separate incidents.[9] Prior to those rather seedy episodes, Cosby embarked on a national tour encouraging black Americans to take more personal responsibility for their conditions and reinforce healthy family values and priorities. Like the staunchest conservative dogma, Cosby made almost no attempt to link black suffering to structural impediments that impinge upon the social, political, and economic progress of people of color and the poor. However, as with Patterson, even when Cosby's arguments' flaws are cited, balanced analysis must conclude that he certainly made points that should at least be considered. It would be shortsighted to throw the proverbial baby out with the bathwater. The Cosby and Patterson debates raise the issue of how black culture is constructed and how the public sphere impacts it. This consideration should not, and does not, begin or end with either critic.

While both Patterson and Cosby deliver analyses that are too culture heavy, certain aspects of black and American culture must be confronted in concert with other social, political, or economic problems before any legitimate resistance to negative trends can be organized or nurtured. The establishment of a modern black public sphere that confronts and resists practices and norms (be they internal or external to the race) contrary to egalitarianism is essential in movement toward this goal.

The Kantian Dilemma, Media, Morality, and Meglomania

One cannot speak of the black public sphere without engaging the impact of Black Entertainment Television (BET)—the first black cable network. Its history has been one marked by admirable conquests as well as disturbing failures. For some time, the network has been subjected to well-deserved criticism about its sociopolitical messages and overall direction. The debate reached a zenith in 2001 when the release of Tavis Smiley as host of the BET Tonight program unleashed a firestorm of criticism and inquiry concerning the political ideology and cultural commitment of BET founder Robert Johnson as well as the future of the network after its sale to media giant Viacom.[10] Unfortunately, what was largely missing from the initial angst-riddled discussions surrounding the popular Smiley's firing was a cogent analysis of what the sale of BET itself signaled with respect to black people's ability to access media outlets and convene forums to publicly discuss substantive issues impacting the black human condition.

While there has been understandable disparagement from some segments of the black community of the first network that [supposedly] solely speaks to black interests being dominated by videos featuring scantily clad women gyrating themselves into oblivion, there has been little attention paid to Johnson's shift from concerns with black culture to his apparent obsession with green capital. The dismissal of Smiley (currently one of black America's leading political voices) called widespread public attention to Johnson's abandonment of people-oriented principles that has possibly been in the works for some time. To be sure, his stated utilitarianism during the early days of BET did not spontaneously combust. Activist Ron Daniels comments:

> Mr. Johnson is widely regarded as one of the most savvy and successful entrepreneurs in Black America, a consummate businessman who has made it clear, however, that he is not particularly concerned with mixing racial and social concerns with business. Ironically, as a social and political activist in Youngstown, Ohio, some years ago, I distinctly remember being called by representatives of a start-up venture called BET to mobilize Black people to demand that the local cable company carry the programming of the embryonic network. Out of a sense of racial pride and social commitment, we did just that, and I am certain that scores of communities across the country did likewise.[11]

Much of the discussion here is necessarily concerned with external as well as self-representation and identification of black people beyond BET. Inarguably, the lion's share of media attention brought to black people—from rappers to athletes to petty thieves—is often negative. This reality forces us to look at the media as one starting point in our continuing examination of African-descended peripheralization. Rarely does media place black reality in a larger context that includes the history and doctrines of America that have marginalized and continue to marginalize the black collective. While blacks are certainly sometimes at fault and deserve negative reporting (as people from all groups do), there is no rational excuse for the dearth of positive images. Media's inclination to overstress black retrograde behavior and suffering happens for several reasons. One reason is pure capitalist economics. American media may not be worthy of absolute public trust, because it has a tendency to sensationalize news in an attempt to increase the sale of papers, magazines, television shows, and movies. This practice inevitably contributes to the disempowerment of meaningful rational discourse.

This stance echoes the social criticism of the media by Jurgen Habermas in *The Structural Transformation of the Public Sphere*. Habermas's examination is important in that it illustrates that media may not be the best place to retrieve unbiased information. While Habermas saw modern media as playing a key role in influencing the technological and social organization of communications, he also believed it should not be trusted, because it panders to political agendas wrought with propaganda and economic manipulation. Central to his argument is the contention that the rise of new media forms (telegraph, telephone, film, and especially television) undermines citizens' discursive relations. The modern individual and family are subjected to regulation of information flow from without because of their lack of critical engagement. In today's cynical society, people often do not come together to discuss and rationally evaluate books, movies, or television programs. Though families may convene to participate in media consumption, very rarely do they subsequently engage in discourse about the core issues presented by (or that are absent from) television shows or films.

This passive consumption blurs line between public and private by allowing both to be colonized by the social. Publicity is lowered amid professionalism as critics become arbiters of taste and decide what is art or trash. Maybe more important, the absence of political discourse often leads to an electorate that is large but basically inactive. In such an environment, representatives gain votes as media stars rather than participants in viable political dialogue with the people. This allows for the reality that most political campaigns are now largely devoid of true political substance. Citizens recognize the emptiness but feel powerless to change it.

Admittedly, maintenance of a viable public sphere is difficult in a political environment sanitized and dumbed by the filtering of the political through popular culture and the visceral, underdeveloped, pseudopolitical engagement that accompanies it. If productive dialogical exchange and clear articulation of issues and agendas *within* liberal space rarely occur, it is almost impossible to alter society into a site of political struggle that is systemically oppositional by presenting alternative possibilities from without. Habermas's concern with the condition of modern political institutions ties the genesis of the bourgeois public sphere to the rise and transformation of capitalism and the state. The very concept of the public sphere assumes that participants have equal access to information and opportunities to participate in the formation and practice of politics.

Ideally, in this framework governing political bodies are open to the people and are true mediums for voicing public opinion. The reality, however, is that these bodies are usually largely closed to the people. Dissemination of information is quite often intentionally stagnated, and the populace cannot engage in truly informed dialogue. The governmental vehicle is thus not truly public when decision-making concerns are brought to bear, but one for the enunciation of preset opinions and the announcement of compromises made behind the scenes by political conspirators (again, whether or not they know they conspire). Media machines are integral to this process in that they often report the symbolic agreements, not the underlying critical issues. Ownership of such media tools in the modern capitalist society is con-centrated, and they are run as profit-making businesses rather than open ideological marketplaces.

Succinctly, the Habermasian public sphere ideally serves as a forum for communication aimed at mutual knowledge and understanding among a democratic society's populace. In the modern era, however, there is a threat to democracy itself by media with purposive agendas usually centering on capitalist gain. By tracing the intellectual history of the core ideas that shape the constitution of the public sphere, Habermas concludes that the entire notion of the public sphere is rooted in the engagement of public opinion, which he believes can be found as early as Hobbes and Locke but reached its fruition in the writ-ings of Immanuel Kant. Kant did not believe public opinion was merely the opinions of individuals of a given society taken in aggregate. Pub-lic opinion was, more substantively, the collective opinion of the masses after personal opinions were subjected to rational-critical, pub-lic discourse. This public interaction, or intersubjectivity, was brought about because of the existence of a thriving civil society. Civil society was only viable, on the Kantian view, if it had the ability to transform private vices into public virtues.

Kant's idea of civil society holding transformative value is largely rooted in his idea of the *categorical imperative*, which has generated a good deal of debate among philosophers. An often-encountered argu-ment against the imperative is that it is nebulous because Kant states it in different ways at different times. Ultimately, the categorical impera-tive can be condensed into two formulations. The first version follows the assertion, "One ought never to act except in such a way that one can also will that one's maxim should become a universal law."[12] Sim-ply put, this interpretation of the categorical imperative purports that an action must be called into moral question if the adoption of the act by everyone in the society could be judged as degenerative or damaging to others or the societal structure itself.

The second version of the categorical imperative is more individ-ually humanistic than the societal-based first one: "Act so that you treat humanity, whether in your own person or that of another, always as an end and never as a means only." The message behind this formu-lation seems to be that "all persons deserve respect simply because they are persons. If this principle is accepted, everyone has a moral duty to treat others fairly and equitably, to refrain from using humans as means for the procurement of one's own or other's ends."[13] Admittedly, Kant's categorical imperative is sometimes unreasonably strict. According to his draconian view of morality, indiscretions—even in the public good—are never excusable. In the real world, such an uncompromising model of morality rarely holds. The formulations of the imperative are relevant, however, in that they provide cogent starting points for constructing bases for moral, social, and political behavior. Certainly, reality demands modifications to Kant. Participants in the public sphere must determine how extensive the adjustments should or should not be. The Kantian dilemma rests on Kant's belief that civil society and the public sphere should transform private vices into public virtues through adherence to the categorical imperative, but they often do not. To be sure, this is the sad reality of the current black public sphere.

Are We What We Wish to Be?

All of us, including Barack Obama, must now wrestle with a number of issues presented by hip-hop as culture. Wrangling over space, place, authenticity, and identity abounds in black America. The troubling issue in the identity-public sphere link is the possibility that the current black public sphere (such as it is) does not transform private vices into public virtues at all but often operates in reverse. What if black mediated spaces are currently wrought with images of the black Self that present and reinforce misogyny, apoliticism, sexual and social frivolity, violence, successive impetuous marriages, hasty divorces, greed, decadence, materialism, and financial exploitation as the norm? At some point, black people must challenge hip-hop along with other factors affecting them and ask: At the end of the day, how do we want our communities to look? Do we want to embrace and expand this approach to the world? Is this who we are? Moreover, if this is who we are, are we what we wish to be?

Admittedly, these questions are laced with moral undertones, and any discussions of morality are plagued by subjective judgment. To admit that the discussion is subjective, however, does not suggest it is crippled by subjectivism.[14] Such a conclusion would necessarily lead to narrow reductionism and traps individuals in a "circle of certainty" that closes them off from serious engagement of opinions contrary to their own. The relative nature of the morality enterprise does, however, plunge discourse surrounding it into very necessary dialogue about who rightfully decides what is moral and what is not. It is here that the essentiality of a generative public sphere can be found. In most cases, even those who argue that right and wrong are relative would not define morality itself out of existence. This is not to say that such extremists cannot be found, but it is to say that to argue the case for morality and virtue with them is nonsensical. Outside of this terrain of amorality, judgments must eventually be made concerning what is good for the progression of the race, and what is not. Ideally, the public sphere is where conversations on this subject play themselves out.

The overriding public sphere concern is where we can locate venues that discuss issues of import to black people and endeavor to humanize their world. In theory, BET was founded to provide a media outlet that would present a myriad of complimentary and competing black images representing the infinite personas and perspectives encountered throughout the black experience. Unfortunately, over the years the network developed into little more than a haven for comic relief, occasional superficial romantic cinema, blaxploitation reruns, and music videos that have increasingly mutated into lightweight pornography. Realistically, BET should not be expected to abandon the music video programming base that secures a good percentage of its audience. The problem lies in the justified argument that, even outside of the videos, the network has largely failed to provide serious programs that speak to issues of cultural, social, and political significance that challenge and counter the often exploitive music. With the failure to construct and cultivate such programming, BET remains true to its name—Black *Entertainment* Television—and nothing more. Unfortunately, many of its viewers seem all too willing to buy into the network's thrust and entertain themselves to death.

This process, as with all hegemonic interactions, involves coercion and consent. As society continues to struggle against *anomie* and confusion over personhood, paths to the construction of positive black identity are largely hidden. Modern America has erected a culture that places inordinate value on materialism, prestige, personal possessions, and wealth. Through this resituating of values, black identity problems are intensified along with those of their fellow Americans. In the modern environment of conspicuous consumption, envy, and greed, the very core of who we are, black or not, has changed.

One clear reason why black elites, inside as well as outside of politics proper, resist serious challenge to capitalism is because they have positioned themselves to be the members of the black community who are most likely to enjoy its fruits. Robert Johnson's activities at BET and beyond are simply isolated examples that lend credence to the statement, "Capitalism is an amoral philosophy, which admits no obligation to social responsibility. Its motive force is profit, property and the acquisition of material wealth by any means possible."[15] Capitalists, black or white, conveniently suffer from selective amnesia when loyalty to the struggle of the masses does not benefit them economically. Staying true to the individualistic greed ethic, a good percentage of the disconnected bourgeoisie applauded Johnson's sale of BET, because it made an astronomical amount of money and reflected his poignancy as an "entrepreneur." What these financially tunnel-visioned people failed to realize was the struggle for economic empowerment should not blind one to the fact that economic struggle does not stand alone in the attempt to construct a collective politics of humanization. In their defense, Johnson's next major venture would have earth-shaking paradigmatic possibilities for the future of black progress: he bought a basketball team (yes, sarcasm intended).

Hip-hop leadership and culture now extend well beyond Johnson, BET, and music. For instance, since 2001 Russell Simmons has spearheaded what he dubs the Hip-Hop Summit Action Network (HSAN). Its mission statement reads:

> The Hip-Hop Summit Action Network (HSAN) is dedicated to harnessing the cultural relevance of Hip-Hop music to serve as a catalyst for education advocacy and other societal concerns fundamental to the empowerment of youth. HSAN is a non-profit, non-partisan national coalition of Hip-Hop artists, entertainment industry leaders, education advocates, civil rights proponents, and youth leaders united in the belief that Hip-Hop is an enormously influential agent for social change which must be responsibly and proactively utilized to fight the war on poverty and injustice.[16]

The organization truly blends hip-hop, politics, and culture. Even though Simmons serves as the group's chairman, its president and CEO is the controversial Benjamin Chavis, former executive director and CEO of the NAACP, who sports a record of more than four decades of civil rights involvement.

HSAN is not the only example of hip-hop's dabblings in politics. During the 2004 presidential election, one of the most popular voter registration initiatives was Sean "Diddy" Combs' "Vote or Die!" campaign. The scene of Combs rubbing shoulders with politicos such as former Democratic National Committee chair Terry McAuliffe was interesting to say the least. Other aspects of Vote or Die! were not simply novel; they were disturbing. For many, a pressing question was not only if Diddy and his associates could promote voter registration among the young (which they clearly did to a degree), but could they also help provide much-needed voter education? The fact that some of the celebrity personalities used to promote Vote or Die! themselves turned out to be unregistered and at times politically uninformed was telling:

> Throughout the election year, both the mainstream media and some grassroots activists criticized celebrity-driven hip hop organizations as sometimes hypocritical in their politics, less than revolutionary, and short-sighted. To be sure, HSAN and "Vote or Die!" were not the heavyweights of voter education. This was most apparent by the faces that fronted the voting campaigns—artists, not organizers, who were sometimes ignorant about the political issues of the 2004 election.

> The New York Times called P. Diddy's campaign "insincere marketing" and made fun of the "trendy T-shirts" that were passed out to newly registered voters. The Boston Globe noted that at a summit in Bean Town, Congresswoman Maxine Waters received "polite applause" from the crowd while musician Lloyd Banks was greeted with "near hysterics." A San Francisco Chronicle writer made fun of HSAN's goal of eliminating poverty, asking "How does that work, if what most mainstream rappers represent is part of the problem in eliminating poverty?"[17]

Today's hip-hop artists and their followers may be riding in a different vehicle, but their driver is the same one who chauffeurs other black leadership communities: the unyielding and unapologetic pursuit of personal, not collective, capital. As Johnson's sale of BET illustrates, in many cases, after economic benefits are garnered at the expense of the black masses, black capitalists desert projects that may benefit them. In many cases, they may never have been committed to the projects at all. Like Johnson, many black American elites become collaborators in the maintenance of permanent hegemony in that, in the name of entrepreneurship, they fight doggedly to maintain capitalist fiefdoms that engender no dedication to social utilitarianism.

In the midst of this fray of greed, black leadership often engages in political and economic competition to determine who has the "right" to become what Freire called "sub-oppressors."[18] These people only further commodify and exploit those occupying society's lower rungs.

Future prospects for constructive black collective progress are bleak if these realities are allowed to stay their courses. The reconstruction of the black public sphere and a generative cultural base that accompanies it are essential battlegrounds where this process will be either interrupted or augmented. Unfortunately, hip-hop leaders and the business moguls who support them seem ill-prepared or unwilling to construct, affirm, and promote constructive movements that demand the cessation of current modes of engagement.

Dangerously, many people are so immersed in hip-hop that some now see hip-hop culture *as* black culture. Of course, it is not. At best, hip-hop is a byproduct of segments of youth and American market culture. Black people are greater than our musical contributions to the world, but even if one limits the argument to music, we are more than hip-hop. We "people who are darker than blue" as Curtis Mayfield called us are not just Lil' Kim. We are also John Coltrane's horn singing pain in "Alabama." We are not just Jadakiss. We are Harold Melvin, Teddy Pendergrass and the Blue Notes begging everybody to "Wake Up." We are not just the Ying Yang Twins. We are the Isleys seeking a "Harvest for the World." We are greater than R. Kelly's water sports and foolishness about flirting and clubbing. We are Stevie Wonder, Sam Cooke, and Marvin Gaye. We are Lady Day. We are Monk. We are Robeson. We are a vanguard people. We are not just hip-hop, and we would do well to remember it.

While we are struggling with our historical memories, we should also note that the rappers are not alone in their attempts to bring the worlds of individualism, materialism, and decadence in their music into reality. They have had good teachers. Today's black politicians, bourgeois educated elites, ministers, professional activists, and business moguls have provided fine examples of how to "get paid" by any means necessary. In this respect, the rappers have learned from other black leadership communities, and, for good or ill, an entire generation of black youth is learning from the rappers. We have yet to understand the full length and breadth of the consequences.

7

What's Wrong with Us?

The Necessary Death of American Romanticism

Think of it as plastic memory, this force within you which trends you and your fellows toward tribal forms. This plastic memory seeks to return to its ancient shape, the tribal society. It is all around you—the feudatory, the diocese, the corporation, the platoon, the sports club, the dance troupes, the rebel cell, the planning council, the prayer group . . . each with its master and servants, its host and parasites. And the swarms of alienating devices (including these words!) tend eventually to be enlisted in the argument for a return to "those better times." I despair of teaching you other ways. You have square thoughts which resist circles.
                    —Frank Herbert, *God Emperor of Dune*

When and where I enter, in the quiet, undisputed dignity of my womanhood, without violence and without suing or special patronage, then and there the whole Negro race enters with me.
                    —Anna Julia Cooper, *A Voice from the South*

I have not failed. I've just found 10,000 ways that won't work.
                    —Thomas Alva Edison (popular quote, unsourced)

In February 2007, Barack Obama supporters gathered in Springfield, Illinois' town square to hear him tell the country what many had suspected for months: that despite past denials, he was indeed officially running for president of the United States. From choosing the location of his announcement to his words, Obama went to considerable lengths to draw comparisons between himself and another Illinois politician, one of his "political heroes," Abraham Lincoln. The linkage was important for Obama because, in his words, Lincoln's work was the reason Americans of every race could "stand together to face the challenges of the 21st century":

> It was here, in Springfield, where North, South, East and West come together that I was reminded of the essential decency of the American people—where I came to believe that through this decency, we can build a more hopeful America. . . . And that is why, in the shadow of the Old State Capitol, where Lincoln once called on a divided house to stand together, where common hopes and common dreams still live, I stand before you today to announce my candidacy for President of the United States of America.[1]

The Obama-Lincoln parallels were not contrived in some respects. Like Lincoln in the late 1850s, Obama was viewed as a novice to national politics in 2007. Both spent eight years in the Illinois state senate and just two in the United States Senate before running for president. Obama lost his first bid for Congress in 2000. Lincoln lost a Senate bid in 1858, two years before being elected president. Interestingly, Lincoln, too, was viewed as ambivalent about the problem of race during his political career.

Lincoln and the Negro Problem

While acknowledging his greatness, Obama would also be well served by not taking on some of Lincoln's baggage. Though the facts are rarely discussed, the legendary Lincoln and the historical Lincoln are not always easily reconciled. For instance, he was not consistently politically committed to freeing America's slaves as many believe. Lincoln apologists argue that he rarely openly expressed his deep-seated antislavery sentiments for strategic reasons. Later in life, Lincoln did indeed proclaim that he "always hated slavery." So maybe playing politics explains his compromises on legislation and refusal to use presidential power to support emancipation prior to 1863. But maybe it does not.

Others argue that Lincoln was never committed to freeing slaves at all but was forced into it as a matter of political expediency during the Civil War. In 1862, while Lincoln was drafting the Emancipation

Proclamation, the *New York Tribune's* Horace Greeley wrote an editorial arguing that the president's goal with regards to slavery should be nothing less than complete abolition. Lincoln responded:

> I would save the Union. I would save it the shortest way under the Constitution. The sooner the national authority can be restored; the nearer the Union will be "the Union as it was." If there be those who would not save the Union, unless they could at the same time save slavery, I do not agree with them. If there be those who would not save the Union unless they could at the same time destroy slavery, I do not agree with them. My paramount object in this struggle is to save the Union, and is not either to save or to destroy slavery.
>
> If I could save the Union without freeing any slave I would do it, and if I could save it by freeing all the slaves I would do it; and if I could save it by freeing some and leaving others alone I would also do that. What I do about slavery and the colored race, I do because I believe it helps to save the Union; and what I forbear, I forbear because I do not believe it would help to save the Union. I shall do less whenever I shall believe what I am doing hurts the cause, and I shall do more whenever I shall believe doing more will help the cause. I shall try to correct errors when shown to be errors; and I shall adopt new views so fast as they shall appear to be true views.
>
> I have here stated my purpose according to my view of official duty; and I intend no modification of my oft-expressed personal wish that all men everywhere could be free.[2]

It is important that while often viewed as an executive order freeing the slaves, the Emancipation Proclamation actually only manumitted slaves in Confederate territories, over which Lincoln had no authority in 1863. In reality, American slavery did not end until 1865 with the passage of the Thirteenth Amendment.

Many rightfully argue that Lincoln's ideal solution to slavery was, in fact, not emancipation and integration of blacks into American society at all, but the deportation and colonization of the country's former slaves. From the 1840s forward, Lincoln was an advocate of the American Colonization Society (ACS) and its program of colonizing free blacks in Liberia. The greatest black leader of the day, Frederick Douglass was deeply opposed to the ACS. His opposition was based on the fact that the ACS was not an abolitionist organization. Indeed, the ACS was dominated by slaveholders and northern antiabolitionists.

Despite the periodic confusion of the ACS with the abolitionist jug-
gernaut American Anti-Slavery Society (AAS), the ACS did not promote abolition at all but rather colonization plans that would rid the
country of free blacks. Douglass saw this as a path that would ultimately
leave black slaves without advocates, leadership, or hope. Lincoln obviously disagreed.

Lincoln's support for colonization did not disappear throughout his
presidency. During his time in office, Lincoln explored any number of
options to deport blacks. He actually appointed a commissioner of emi-
gration to oversee colonization projects in 1861.[3] Between 1861 and
1862 Lincoln actively negotiated contracts with businessmen to colo-
nize freed blacks in Panama and on a small island off the coast of Haiti.
The Haiti plan collapsed in 1863. The much larger Panama contract
ran aground the same year after the government of Colombia objected.
In 1862, Lincoln also convened a colonization conference at the White
House where he addressed a group of free blacks, attempting to convince them to support his colonization ideas.

Despite the Panama and Haiti failures, Lincoln continued to advocate colonization during his second term. A short time before his death
in 1865, he met with General Benjamin F. Butler and talked of export-
ing blacks:

> What shall we do with the Negroes after they are free? . . . I can
> hardly believe that the South and North can live in peace unless we
> can get rid of the Negroes. . . . I believe that it would be better to
> export them all to some fertile country with a good climate, which
> they could have to themselves. If these black soldiers of ours go back
> to the South, I am afraid that they will be but little better off with
> their masters than they were before, and yet they will be free men. I
> fear a race war, and it will be at least a guerilla war because we have
> taught these men how to fight. . . . There are plenty of men in the
> North who will furnish the Negroes with arms if there is any oppres-
> sion of them by their late masters.[4]

Charles Wesley concludes, "Although Lincoln believed in the
destruction of slavery, he desired the complete separation of the
whites and blacks. Throughout his political career, Lincoln persisted
in believing in the colonization of the Negro."[5] Luckily, as Barack
Obama embarked upon his first presidential candidacy, he would not
have to wrestle with the issue of slavery. He would, however, have to
deal with its legacy.

We Must Be What We Were: Rewriting the Script of Struggle

At the end of the day, Obama's greatest challenge when dealing with black Americans will be balancing their legitimate quest for leadership that speaks to their concerns and the illegitimate and unhealthy yearning for a savior. Examination of current post–civil rights black leadership—from politicians to ministers to musicians to media moguls to the educated elite—clearly illustrates change is sorely needed. In many ways our assessment here has been a continuation of the projects of Robert Smith and Ronald Walters, Harold Cruse, William Banks, and others. By its very title, Smith and Walter's important *We Have No Leaders* is self-explanatory. Of course, they do not contend that black people have *no* leaders; they simply believe we have *bad* ones. Smith and Walters study the political aftermath of the civil rights movement by exploring events spanning back to the Montgomery bus boycott of 1955. They ultimately conclude that post–civil rights African American political movements have been coopted by the main, due to regressive political traditions of black leadership and the overall decay of the black community.

Harold Cruse would probably disagree with the assertion that black movements *became* coopted. According to his lambasting of the lion's share of twentieth-century black leadership in *Crisis of the Negro Intellectual*, most movements were always controlled by core-group forces more than blacks care to admit. To be sure, there is a paralyzing level of romanticism about the past and nihilism about the future in black America. Barack Obama and every leader of darker hue will inevitably be impacted by both. On the 2008 presidential campaign trail, Obama himself often proclaimed his toughest opponent was "cynicism."

Past and present continue to wrestle in black America. Older, traditional civil rights–type leaders are still present in most places. The older generation is sometimes aided, but often challenged, by a new cadre of would-be leaders labeling themselves "community activists." This new breed frequently approaches advocacy as a profession, not a calling—often not maintaining employment outside of it. Some regard these new activists as so utterly dedicated to solving the problems of their communities that they cannot pursue traditional careers. Others see them as little more than money-grubbing, manipulative hustlers who prey on black suffering. It is activism as business: it pays. Both perspectives are probably true in different cases.

Understandably, most of these men outwardly model themselves on Martin Luther King Jr. Ironically, more than anyone, King carved out space for this new crop of local and national celebrity activists. Toward the end of his life, he anticipated their bastardization of his legacy, but the epiphany came too late. In the last installment of his three-volume biography of King, At Canaan's Edge, Taylor Branch recounts that shortly before his death King lamented that "[Andrew] Young had given in to doubt, [James] Bevel to brains, and [Jesse] Jackson to ambition. He said they had forgotten the simple truths of witness. . . . [T]he movement had made them, and now they were using the movement to promote themselves."[6] Since King's death, this trend has continued.

Usually, both the civil rights leaders and new community activists have some religious affiliation, tossing the "Reverend" or "Minister" titles about, which, as we have seen, effectively garner trust from many blacks. It is important that neither offers strategies for proactive sociopolitical empowerment—more often than not reacting to single, blatant instances of disrespect or death. These cases are usually spoken to by tiny coalitions of less influential ministers; NAACP representatives; and small, little known local activist organizations. A typical gathering, harkening to the civil rights era, usually includes speeches, prayers, religious song, and maybe a protest march to bring a moment of comfort to affected populations. Unfortunately, no matter how well-intentioned, little progressive political strategy is proffered because these protest gatherings are regarded as both beginnings and ends. At the end of the day, blacks on the ground are left in the same condition they were in before the meetings, marches, and prayers.

As strategy-poor and ineffective as these leadership communities are, they maintain their positions among blacks largely because of suffering itself. It is a dismal cycle. Racial hegemony creates black suffering; black suffering prompts perceptions of insurmountable disempowerment; disempowerment breeds dependence; dependence often fosters weakness; and weakness enables the continuance of hegemony. This interaction necessarily lowers both masses and leaders over time. The fact that overly dependent masses often find comfort in ignorance and never take an active role in struggles to better their worlds plagues leaders with decent intent. Power and position often seduce some of these leaders, and they lose their way, but the rare ones who stay the course are inevitably susceptible to loneliness, burnout, and easy targeting by opponents.

Abusive leaders use collective weakness bred by dependency for their own gain. This is the path set upon by many of today's ministers and community activists. Financial gain, masked by rhetoric of justice

and healing, is the goal. Their influence rests firmly upon the reification among the masses that a satisfactory future requires a return to an
idealized past—a past that, in fact, never existed. To be sure, many in
the black community mythologize the civil rights era as a time everyone was involved in struggle, and ministers and civil rights organizations single-handedly "led us to freedom." Other blacks extend this pattern to idealizing segregation, the strength of racial purity, and even
Africa. Of course, these beliefs are flawed, but the actual historical facts
do not matter.

Admittedly, representative democracy, by its very nature, demands
a certain level of dependency among its citizenry. It relies on elected
officials in particular and other public leaders in general. Ideally, the
expectation in such a political system is that citizens *know* even if they
are not able to *do*—if doing is defined by directly deciding the course of
public policy. This reality is one of political dependency but not necessarily weakness. However, if citizens degenerate to the point where they
neither *do* nor *know*, they are not only dependent but also weak and
open to manipulation. Manipulated people wedded to past-oriented
romanticism are blind to the necessity of developing modern, complex,
political solutions to complex political problems. Coupled with weak,
retrograde leadership this reality leaves much to be desired in post–civil
rights black America. It should come as no surprise that many black people are anxious to crown the next King: a new "savior-leader" to remedy
their ills. It is an unenviable position, and whether Barack Obama
chooses to assume this weight or shun it, there is a price to be paid.

Increasing threats to democratic ideals and liberatory humanization in the United States and beyond make aimless, emotive rants by
ministers and professional activists less and less relevant. The focus
must be broader, clearer, and more inclusive as the American landscape
shifts. This means that, even though black folk are comfortable with
them, old approaches now must be reexamined, augmented, and sometimes discarded. This is a troubling proposition, because it forces us out
of familiar zones of comfort. Increasingly, we are in need of people who
have skill sets that move beyond superficial (and often flawed) commentaries on ontological realities and interrogate epistemological reasons behind them. Only then can we grasp new and innovative paradigmatic possibilities that stand greater chances of bringing something
more beautiful and just into the world.

We must engage and seek to balance many factors that face us
daily: individual cultural debauchery against systemic oppression; the
criminality of our youth against the criminalization of our people; the

prophetic voices of our holy men against the hubris and nasty exploitation of many of the same; praise of the success of our middle class
against oft-encountered vulgar careerism and disdain toward the less
fortunate; necessary activism against people who profit from the pain of
others. At his best, Barack Obama may provide such a balance. At his
worst, he may not even try. In either case, because he has emerged at
this particular moment in history, Obama will be forced to deal with
unrealistic expectations and sometimes unfair critiques. One of the first
he had to deal with within the black community was angst about his
ethnicity and racial loyalty.

One residual of America's "peculiar institution" is how the country
in general and blacks in particular handle ethnic and racial categoriza-
tion. Of course, white Americans have also dealt with deep-seated ethnic conflict historically. Because of the dominance of strict racial
dichotomization in American society, however, blacks were more often
than not lumped under one grand umbrella leaving little room for ethnic cleavages. For the first time on the national political stage, the
ascendancy of Obama pushed the issue of ethnic identity and racial
authenticity to the fore in black America.

Yes, Barack Obama Is Black Enough, But . . .

Though inevitable, the debate about whether Barack Obama was
"black enough" to garner widespread black electoral support began
shortly before he formally announced his presidential candidacy. Sitting at the heart of the storm was New York Daily News columnist, cultural critic, and contrarian Stanley Crouch. In November 2006,
Crouch commented:

> So when black Americans refer to Obama as "one of us," I do not
> know what they are talking about. In his recent book, The Audacity
> of Hope, Obama makes it clear that, while he has experienced some
> light versions of typical racial stereotypes, he cannot claim those
> problems as his own—nor has he lived the life of a black American.

> Will this matter in the end? Probably not. Obama is being greeted
> with the same kind of public affection that Colin Powell had when
> he seemed ready to knock Bill Clinton out of the Oval Office. For
> many reasons, most of them personal, Powell did not become the first
> black American to be a serious presidential contender. I doubt

Obama will share Powell's fate, but if he throws his hat in the ring, he will have to run as the son of a white woman and an African immigrant. If we then end up with him as our first black president, he will have come into the White House through a side door—which might, at this point, be the only one that's open.[7]

Defending Obama in *Time*, Orlando Patterson called views such as Crouch's a new black American "nativism." He reported that a *Washington Post*–ABC poll taken immediately after Obama declared his candidacy in February 2007 showing him trailing Hillary Clinton by a staggering forty percentage points among black American potential voters might be the result of the possibility that "black Americans have transcended racial politics and may now vote for the person they consider the better candidate, regardless of race."[8] Patterson, however, suspected that something more sinister was amiss. He observed that over time a shift has happened in black American culture that moved it away from open-minded cosmopolitanism to a disturbingly different place.

To their credit, according to Patterson, a native West Indian, black Americans turned the infamous white American "one-drop rule" to their own designs:

> What to racist whites was a stain of impurity became a badge of pride. More significantly, what for whites was a means of exclusion was transformed by blacks into a glorious principle of inclusion. . . . Like so many other West Indians, I have personally experienced this remarkable inclusiveness in the traditional practice of black identity. Becoming a black American meant simply declaring oneself to be one and engaging in their public and private life, into which I was always welcomed.

Patterson then laments that this tradition is now dead in some sectors of black America:

> In recent years, however, this tradition has been eroded by a thickened form of black identity that, sadly, mirrors some of the worst aspects of American white identity and racism. A streak of nativism rears its ugly head. To be black American, in this view, one's ancestors must have been not simply slaves but American slaves. Furthermore, directly mirroring the traditional definition of whiteness as not being black is the growing tendency to define blackness in negative terms—it is to be not white in upbringing, kinship or manner, to be too at ease in the intimate ways of white Americans.[9]

The thoughts of both Crouch and Patterson merit attention. It could certainly be argued, though, that both of their conclusions are flawed. Patterson's supposed nativism simply may not be as pronounced in black America as he contends. More than likely it is not at the heart of many blacks' caution where Obama is concerned. To be fair, whether one tosses ideas of nativism, ethnic identity, or racial responsibility into the public sphere, Obama will suffer from much that is not his fault.

Countering Crouch, no matter his ethnicity, Barack Obama is black. He has never attempted to deny that reality. The fact that he cannot change his "paint job" forces him into the ring as the latest man expected to carry the burden of "savior-leader." He cannot hold up under its weight, of course. The expectations are simply too high. For Barack Obama's sake as well as our own, we must not romanticize him. If black America (or any other segment of the country for that matter) wants a messiah, he will not be able to satisfy them. However, if expectations are radically lowered, he may suffice. We must be clear about what he is and what he is not.

By all accounts, Barack Obama is an intelligent, well-educated man with limitless potential. However, he does not seem to be what Du Bois envisioned when he spoke of a racially committed, selfless Talented Tenth (or Guiding Hundredth). He is clearly a capable, hardworking, charismatic politician. But he is no "Black Hawk" like Adam Clayton Powell Jr., Shirley Chisholm, or Cynthia McKinney. This fact, not black American nativism as Orlando Patterson suggests, will cost Obama black votes in some quarters. Many (not all) black voters are now sophisticated enough to not support a person simply because of race. As we have seen, with shifting ideologies among new black politicians, being black by no means ensures commitment to matters of race.

At a time when black people still face incredibly daunting problems on a number of fronts, many are highly disturbed that most politicians, including Obama, rarely speak to these troubles. Undoubtedly, he should not run a state or national campaign in which he only addresses black issues. That would be foolish. However, he should also not expect blanket black support if he becomes viewed as a candidate who often takes the opportunity to distance his agenda from difficulties hampering black progress.

During his 2008 presidential bid, Obama was avid about health care, alternatives to Middle Eastern oil, and removing American troops from Iraq. All noble endeavors. However, he was firm in his stand that race was not his "main focus . . . if there are symbolic benefits from it, that's great."[10] In an interview with National Public

Radio, Obama acknowledged, "In the history of African-American pol-itics in this country there has always been some tension between speak-ing in universal terms and speaking in very race-specific terms about the plight of the African-American community. By virtue of my back-ground, I am more likely to speak in universal terms."[11]

Obama is a man quite comfortable speaking of his religious faith and its place in politics. He is not, however, a man who will step into black communities and speak out against exploitive celebrity preachers or cut them off at the knees by stopping political funding for question-able religious endeavors. While he certainly appeals to some of Amer-ica's young, and despite his appearance on an August 2007 cover of *Vibe* magazine declaring, "It's Obama Time," Obama has shown little to lead us to believe he has any interest in connecting with or reshaping the dis-affected parts of hip-hop culture that function on the margins of society.

If Obama is expected to wholly commit himself to championing policies that will finally destroy American racial hegemony and pro-duce an egalitarian society in which black folk can fully participate, he more than likely will fail. For all his talent, he simply does not seem to have the stomach for that fight. If he is allowed to pick low-hanging fruit like other American politicians and leave the country in close to the same condition he found it, he will do just fine. He is no Frederick Douglass, Charles Hamilton Houston, or Martin King Jr. For good or ill, he does not seem to aspire to those heights. Barack Obama is black, but he is not a "race man." He is not a black leader but an American leader who happens to be black. Black America would do well to accept these realities.

Beyond the often disappointing realities surrounding Obama and "Obamamania," the question, What's wrong with Barack Obama? is an intriguing double-entendre. If read, What's *wrong* with Barack Obama? we interrogate the man, which is needed of course. What are his short-comings? Will he do what we think he should? Will he give us what we need? Is he worthy of the hype and our emotional investment? Con-versely, What's wrong with *Barack Obama*? takes us down a different path. That question forces us to ask, "What's wrong with us?" It pushes America, its ideals, its citizenry, and many of its disquieting realities into the spotlight. It is a much more difficult query.

By February 2008, Obama was locked in a no holds barred battle with Hillary Clinton for the Democratic presidential nomination. A lit-tle more than a year after his announcement at Springfield, Obama moved into the position of Democratic front-runner. In a race that was so close that it could possibly be decided by Democratic "super delegates" or a brokered national convention, many believed Obama was poised to become America's first African-American president. To be sure, even if he fell in defeat very few believed this would be his last foray into presidential politics. This fact leads us to close as we began, with a few questions. They are also intriguing. Would Barack Obama be any less of a president than his competitors? Probably not. Is that saying much? Considering most of the competition, no. Is he smart, informed, strategic, and tough enough to be president? Definitely. Would he be a good president? Probably. Would he be a great one? Possibly. Will some white Americans *not* vote for him because he is black? Absolutely. Will enough Americans put their racial baggage aside and cast their lot with "the skinny guy with the funny name" who happens to be black and deliver him to the Oval Office at any point in his political career? We shall see. Then the next phase of our progress—or regress—begins. In the meantime, I will be here—still worrying.

Chronology

Development and Change in Black Leadership Communities from 1619 to Present

Preabolition Era (1619–1865)

- Preinternational Slave Trade Close Abolitionist (1619–1807)
- Postinternational Slave Trade Abolitionist (1808–1865)
- Religious (AME Church; others follow)

Reconstruction Era (1865–1877)

- Religious
- Political/Elected
- Overarching Postabolitionist

Postreconstruction Era (1877–1895)

- Religious
- Overarching Postreconstruction
- Educational-Administrative

Premodern Civil Rights Era (1895–1954)

- Religious
- Civil/Human Rights
- Educational-Administrative
- Entertainment/Athletic
- Business (Individual)

- Political/Elected
- Intellectual
- Artistic Intellectuals
- Media (Print)

Modern Civil Rights Era (1954–1968)

- Religious
- Civil/Human Rights
- Educational-Administrative
- Media

- Political/Elected
- Intellectual
- Artistic Intellectuals
- Business (Small)

Postmodern Civil Rights Era (1968–Present) Radical Paradigm Shift

- Religious (Megachurch variant)
- Political/Elected (percentage ideologically moved to center or right)
- Social/Community Activist (civil rights as business variant)
- Intellectual (migrated from HBCUs to elite schools)
- Educational-Administrative (retreated from forefront)
- Business (dominated by corporate variant)
- Entertainers (dominated by hip-hop variant)
- Entertainment Moguls (Emergent)
- Media (Actor/Television Personalities)

Notes

Foreword

1. Patricia Hill Collins, *Black Sexual Politics: Black Americans, Gender and the New Racism* (New York: Routledge, 2004); J. Blaine Hudson, "Affirmative Action and American Racism in Historical Perspective," *The Journal of Negro History* 84.3 (1999) 260–74.

2. Cecelia A. Conrad, John Whitehead, Patrick Mason, and James Stewart, eds., *African Americans in the U. S. Economy* (New York: Rowman and Littlefield, 2005).

3. World Bank, *World Development Indicators, 2006*. CD-Rom (Washington, DC, 2006).

4. J. Blaine Hudson, "Diversity, Inequality and Community: African Americans in American Society," in Philip Alperson, *Diversity and Community: An Interdisciplinary Reader* (New York: Blackwell, 2003).

5. W. E. B. Du Bois, *The Education of Black People: Ten Critiques, 1906–1960*, ed. Herbert Aptheker (Amherst: University of Massachusetts Press, 1973).

6. For a good analysis of "authentic blackness," see Howard Winant, *The New Politics of Race: Globalism, Difference, Justice* (Minneapolis: University of Minnesota Press, 2004).

1. A Series of Unfortunate (and Unsavory) Events: Paving the Way for "Obamamania"

1. Marsalis' piece entitled "Saving America's Soul Kitchen: How to Bring this Country Together? Listen to the Message of New Orleans," was published in the September 12, 2005, issue of *Time*.

2. Brian Faler, "Bennett under Fire for Remark on Crime and Black Abortions," *Washington Post*, September 30, 2005: A5. Many called for Bennett's dismissal after the comments. He was not fired. In fact, Bennett was also hired as a political analyst by CNN after conservative pundit Robert Novak left the network for rival Fox News in December 2005.

3. Andrew McCarthy, "Shameful Attacks: Bill Bennett Stresses Our Morality . . . and Pays the Price," *National Review Online*, http://www.nationalreview.com/mccarthy/mccarthy200509301104.asp (September 30, 2005)

4. Courtland Milloy, "Sorry Black America, Bennett Isn't Your Problem," *Washington Post*, October 5, 2005.

5. "New Orleans Man—I Wasn't Drunk: Retired School Teacher Says He's Baffled By Police Beating," *CBS News/Associated Press* (October 10, 2005).

6. Jill Lawrence, "Ohio Republican tied to ex-lobbyist scraps House run," *USA Today*, August 7, 2006.

7. Robert B. Edgerton, *The Troubled Heart of Africa: A History of the Congo* (New York: St. Martin's, 2002) 180–81.

8. Cal Thomas, "Who's the Racist?" *Jewish World Review*, August 22, 2006.

9. Abigail Goldman, "Young to Quit Wal-Mart after Racial Remarks," *Los Angeles Times*, August 18, 2006: A1.

10. Thomas Edsall, "Lott Decried for Part of Salute to Thurmond: GOP Senate Leader Hails Colleague's Run as Segregationist," *Washington Post*, December 7, 2002: A6.

11. Dana Bash and Kimberly Segal, "Colleague: We Told Foley to Stop Contacting Teen," *CNN.com*, September 30, 2006.

12. Johnathan Wiseman, "Lawmaker Saw Foley Messages in 2000: Page Notified GOP Rep. Kolbe," *CNN.com*, October 9, 2006.

13. See John Chase and Liam Ford, "Ryan File a Bombshell: Ex-wife Alleges GOP Candidate Took Her to Sex Clubs," *Chicago Tribune*, June 22, 2004, and Liam Ford and Rudolph Bush, "Ryan Quits Race: State GOP Scrambles to Find Replacement to Face Obama; Republican Senate nominee cites fixation on divorce files," *Chicago Tribune*, June 26, 2004.

14. *Tavis Smiley Show*, "Cornel West: Missing Items from Democratic National Committee Agenda," August 4, 2004.

15. Program on International Policy Attitudes, "The Separate Realities of Bush and Kerry Supporters: Bush Supporters Still Believe Iraq Had WMD or Major Program, Supported al-Qaeda," October 21, 2004.

16. West made these comments on National Public Radio's *Tavis Smiley Show* on November 10, 2004.

17. Blacks overwhelmingly supported John Kerry with 88 percent of their vote.

18. Jeffrey H. Reiman, *In Defense of Political Philosophy* (New York: Harper Torchbooks, 1972) xiii–xiv.

19. Morris Berman, *The Twilight of American Culture* (New York: Norton, 2000) 19. In late 2006, in fact, yet another "Rocky" movie, *Rocky Balboa,* was released.

20. "Putin: U.S. Oushing Others into Nuclear Ambition," *Associated Press,* February 10, 2007.

21. Ibid.

22. Cal Thomas, "Barack Obama: American Idol," *Jewish World Review,* January 18, 2007.

23. *Tavis Smiley Show,* "Public Radio International," August 4, 2004.

24. Kenneth Meeks, "Backtalk with Scholar Dr. Cornel West," *Black Enterprise,* February 2005.

2. Sorry, Du Bois Doesn't Live Here Anymore: The Soulessness of the New Talented Tenth

1. Douglas O. Linder, "Before Brown: Charles H. Houston and the Gaines Case," http://www.law.umkc.edu/faculty/projects/ftrials/trialheroes/charleshoustonessayF.html (2000).

2. Ibid.

3. Booker T. Washington, "Atlanta Exposition Address," excerpted from Molefi Asante and Abu Abarry, *African Intellectual Heritage* (Philadelphia: Temple, 1996).

4. In this context, critical consciousness speaks to the ability of an agent to engage in rational evaluation (critical thinking) and action after reflection (praxis). *Critical* thinking must be emphasized, because uncritical thinking does not have the same liberating potential. Consequently, even if a nonthinker acts he/she is not engaged in praxis, because without reflection his/her actions are not truly self-determined, but dictated from without. Finally, critical thinking without eventually engaging reality through acting to change it is also not liberating.

5. Paulo Freire, *Pedagogy of the Oppressed* (New York: Continuum, 1970) 58, 60.

6. Ibid. 58.

7. The phrase was actually created by white liberal Henry Lyman Morehouse for whom Morehouse College is named. Morehouse was the executive

secretary of the American Home Missionary Society. It is believed Morehouse deployed the phrase in 1896 largely in response to the educational ideologies of Booker T. Washington and his "Atlanta Exposition Address" delivered the previous year. Morehouse College was renamed in honor of Henry Morehouse during John Hope's tenure as the college's president (1906–1930). Hope also openly opposed what he saw as Washington's overemphasis on vocational and agricultural education.

8. Herbert J. Storing, ed., *What Country Have I? Political Writings of Black Americans* (New York: St. Martin's, 1970) 102.

9. Ibid.

10. Ibid.

11. Ibid.

12. See Karl Marx and Frederick Engels, *The Manifesto of the Communist Party* (Peking: Foreign Languages Press, 1965), and Bernard Susser, *Political Ideology in the Modern World* (Needham Heights, MA: Allyn and Bacon, 1995).

13. Storing, *What Country Have I?* 103.

14. It should be noted that Du Bois' emphasis on European culture here is case specific. Much of his work glorified Africa and its legacy to an almost unparalleled degree. In the case of Talented Tenth theory, however, this glorification is largely absent.

15. Joy James, *Transcending the Talented Tenth: Black Leaders and American Intellectuals* (New York: Routledge) 23.

16. See David Levering Lewis, ed., *W. E. B. Du bois: A Reader* (New York: Holt, 1995).

17. W. E. B Du Bois, *Dusk of Dawn: An Essay toward an Autobiography of a Race Concept* (New York: Shocker 1940; reprinted 1968) 217.

18. Lewis, *W. E. B. Du Bois: A Reader* 348.

19. Ibid. 349.

20. Contrary to what is often assumed, Freire did not invent the term *conscientization*. But like Du Bois did with the term *Talented Tenth*, Freire popularized it. The word had previously appeared in France, and Freire heard of it through his interaction with intellectuals associated with the Instituto Superior de Etudos Brasileiros. The word eventually fell into disfavor with Freire, because he felt it had been coopted by mainstream educational structures in an attempt to preserve the status quo. Consequently, he stopped using it altogether in the early seventies.

21. The first stage of consciousness is semi-intransitivity, because total intransitivity (complete disconnection from the outside world) is not considered a form of consciousness at all.

22. Tom Heaney, "Issues in Freirean Pedagogy," http://nlu.nl.edu/ace/Resources/Documents/Freire.html.

23. Ibid.

24. Ibid.

25. Freire, *Pedagogy of the Oppressed* 59.

26. Heaney, "Issues in Freirean Pedagogy."

27. Freire, *Pedagogy of the Oppressed* 63.

28. Heaney, "Issues in Freirean Pedagogy."

29. William Banks, *Black Intellectuals* (New York: Norton 1996) 225.

30. Ibid.

31. Patricia Williams, "L'Etranger," *The Nation* (March 5, 2007): 14.

3. The Witch and the Devil:
American Political Philosophy and Black Suffering

1. Fine examinations of consensus formation can be found in Todd Gitlin, *The Whole World Is Watching: Mass Media and the Making and Unmaking of the New Left* (Berkeley: University of California 1980); Jeffery Goldfarb, *The Cynical Society: The Culture of Politics and the Politics of Culture in American Life* (Chicago: University of Chicago Press, 1991); Lawrence Grossberg, *We Gotta Get Outta This Place* (New York: Routledge 1992).

2. Valentino Gerratana, *Antonio Gramsci: Quaderni del carcere* (Turin: Einaudi: 1975) 130.

3. Marx engages this progression and its consequences in *Capital* (New York: Modern Library, 1936), as well as the classic *Manifesto of the Communist Party* (Garden City, NY: Doubleday Anchor, 1959), coauthored with Friedrich Engels.

4. In Bernard Susser, *Political Ideology in the Modern World* (Needham Heights, MA: Allyn and Bacon, 1995) 121.

5. After a half century of civil war, James II was replaced (upon invitation) by William and Mary of Orange. Once they assumed the role of king and queen of England, they accepted a Bill of Rights that gave Parliament sovereign power over English government. This act came to be known as the bloodless or Glorious Revolution. Louis Hartz, *The Liberal Tradition in America* (New York: Harcourt, 1955), and Theodore Lowi, *The End of Liberalism* (New York: Norton, 1979), are fine studies of American liberalism.

6. Susser, *Political Ideology in the Modern World* 59.

7. Lucius Barker, Mack Jones, and Katherine Tate, *African Americans and the American Political System* (New Jersey: Prentice Hall, 1999) 59.

8. Classical liberalism advocates minimal government, absolute property rights, and laissez-faire economics. Welfare liberalism holds the view that only through government intervention in the marketplace can the initial aims of liberalism be preserved.

9. Susser, *Political Ideology in the Modern World* 58.

10. Gabriel Kolko, *Wealth and Power in America* (New York: Praeger, 1962) 14–20.

11. Barker, Jones, and Tate, *African Americans and the American Political System* 57.

12. Ibid.

13. Ibid. 58.

14. Lawrence Grossberg, *We Gotta Get Outta This Place: Popular Conservatism and Postmodern Culture* (New York: Routledge 1992) 247.

15. Ibid. 246–47.

16. The protests of various Florida canvassing boards after the 2000 presidential election (which some believe contributed to the decision to cease the initial vote recount in Miami-Dade County) by Republican supporters, many of whom were imported into Florida, is a good example of such orchestration.

17. Grossberg, *We Gotta Get Outta This Place* 243.

18. Marcus Pohlman, *Black Politics in Conservative America* (New York: Longman 1999) 17–19.

19. *Black Elected Officials: A National Roster, 1993* (Washington, DC: Joint Center for Political and Economic Studies Press 1993) xxii.

20. Barker, Jones, and Tate, *African Americans and the American Political System* 291.

21. Ibid.; Linda Williams, "White-Black Perceptions of the Electability of Black Political Candidates," *National Political Science Review* 2 (1990): 45—64.

22. As noted earlier, incarceration statistics indicate that nearly 50 percent of the national prison population is black male. When the incarcerated Latino and Hispanic population is included, this number expands to over 70 percent. Many of these prisoners are housed in facilities located in rural, white areas. Interestingly, while those convicted of felonies lose their right to vote (even after their release) in many states, they are included in census counts which are used to determine legislative redistricting and reapportionment. In effect, in areas where these prisons are located white political representation is strengthened by counting disenfranchised, imprisoned minorities as potential voters. Serious further examination of this progression must be undertaken in the future.

23. Manning Marable, *Race, Reform, and Rebellion: The Second Reconstruction in Black America, 1945–1982* (Jackson: University of Mississippi Press, 1989) 209.

24. Saul Alinsky, *Rules for Radicals* (New York: Vintage Books, 1971) 11.

25. Marable, *Race, Reform, and Rebellion* 208–09.

4. "Black Hawks" Down: America's War on Terror and the Rise of Bushism

1. McKinney retook the seat two years later when Majette vacated it to pursue an ill-fated run for one of Georgia's U.S. Senate seats. In 2006, after a number of controversies, including striking a Capitol Police security guard, McKinney lost again in the Democratic primary to a different opponent.

2. In an unusual development for a political novice, Majette was able to raise over $1.1 million, nearly twice the money incumbent McKinney had at her disposal.

3. Lynette Clemetson, "For Black Politicians, Two Races Suggest a Rise of New Tactics," *New York Times*, August 22, 2002.

4. Ibid.

5. Ibid.

6. Ibid.

7. The ostracization of McKinney by members of Atlanta's black community extended beyond voters to some of the city's political elites. The most notable of these was former United States ambassador and Atlanta mayor Andrew Young. Young seemed to be so adamant about distancing himself from McKinney that after she claimed to have his endorsement, he refuted her statement by saying that his support was for a previous election—not this one. Long-standing Georgia state representative Tyrone Brooks (who did support McKinney) allowed an Atlanta reporter to listen to a telephone message left by McKinney in which she lamented, "I'm disappointed by your brother Andrew Young, who has left me hanging out there."

8. Jim Galloway, "Outspoken Democrat McKinney Ousted after 10 Years in Congress," *Atlanta Journal-Constitution*, August 21, 2002.

9. Ibid.

10. Hilliard lost his seat to Artur Davis earlier in the summer of 2002. The Hilliard case, while having similarities to McKinney's, is not as compelling because an argument can certainly be made that Hilliard's chances were irreparably damaged by his own history of ethical lapses. For example, in the summer of 2000 Hilliard was rebuked by the House Ethics Committee for converting campaign gifts to his own use. McKinney never subjected her constituents to such behavior.

11. More than 250 violent incidents targeting students of Middle Eastern descent and Islamic religious affiliation on American college campuses were

reported in the first week alone following the bombings. Off campus, a plethora of attacks were levied upon other citizens and visitors including the cold-blooded murder of a citizen of Middle Eastern descent in Mesa, Arizona.

12. This angle is reconsidered later when we engage American foreign policy with respect to the bombings.

13. Black Radical Congress press release, "Terror Attacks of September 11, 2001."

14. Noam Chomsky, "On the Bombings," http://www.zmag.org/chomnote.htm, September 13, 2001.

15. This is true even though many know that examination of line item budgets reveals that the military has been guilty of shady doings such as the purchase four-hundred-dollar toilet seats and dumping fuel off navy ships in the world's oceans, and so on, in an effort to keep the budget from being cut. The long-standing antiaugmentation stance has purported that defense did not need more money but needed to use its existing funds differently. This opinion will now, in the face of national fear, more than likely be all but destroyed.

16. Ibid.

17. Lawrence Grossberg, *We Gotta Get Outta This Place* (New York: Routledge, 1992) 245.

18. Stuart Hall addresses the effects of Thatcherism in a number of works, including *The Hard Road to Renewal: Thatcherism and the Crisis of the Left* (London: Verso, 1988) and "The Toad in the Garden: Thatcherism among the Theorists," in Nelson and Grossberg, eds., *Marxism and the Interpretation of Culture* (Urbana: University of Illinois Press, 1988).

19. Grossberg, *We Gotta Get Outta This Place* 249.

20. Ibid. 267.

21. Ibid. 258.

22. Ibid. 296.

5. I Don't Care What Jesus Would Do; I've Got to Get Paid: The New Black Preacher

1. Jacob Weisberg, "The Path to Power," *Men's Vogue*, October 23, 2006: 220.

2. Ibid.

3. Ibid.

4. David Broder, "God and John McCain," *Washington Post Writers' Group* in *The Courier-Journal*, February 20, 2000: D3.

5. Ibid.

6. Lucius Barker, Mack Jones, and Katherine Tate, *African Americans and the American Political System* (New Jersey: Prentice Hall, 1999) 239.

7. Ibid.

8. Rupe Simms, "Christ Is Black with a Capital 'B'": African American Christianity and the Black Studies Project," *Western Journal of Black Studies* 1.2 (2000): 105.

9. Delores Williams, *Sisters in the Wilderness: The Challenge of Womanist God-Talk* (New York: Orbis, 1998) 206.

10. Ibid. 208.

11. Simms, "Christ Is Black with a Capital 'B'" 106.

12. Murray Stedman, *Religion and Politics in America* (New York: Harbinger, 1964) 22.

13. Pamela Howell, "Clergy Politicians," *Atlanta Good Life*, February, 2001: 11.

14. Ibid. 10.

15. Ibid. 11.

16. Ibid.

17. Cornel West, *Race Matters* (Boston: Beacon, 1992) 11–12.

18. Kevin Cosby, "What Gingrich and the GOP have to offer African-Americans," *The Courier-Journal*, July, 19, 1998: D4.

19. Edward Green, "Fight for Freedom Not Done; Crowd Told Service Marks Anniversary of Emancipation," *The Courier-Journal*, January 2, 2000: B1.

20. Cosby, "What Gingrich and the GOP Have to Offer African-Americans" D4.

21. Ibid.

22. Howell, "Clergy Politicians" 11.

23. Clayborne Carson and Peter Holloran, eds., *A Knock at Midnight: Inspiration from the Great Sermons of Reverend Martin Luther King, Jr.* (New York: Warner Books, 1998) 210–11.

24. Molefi Asante and Abu Abarry, eds., *African Intellectual Heritage: A Book of Sources* (Philadelphia: Temple University Press, 1996) 190.

25. W. E. B. Du Bois, *The Gift of Black Folk* (New York: Washington Square,1970) 65.

26. Ibid. 67.

27. John Fountain, "No Place for Me: I Still Love God, gut I've Lost Faith in the Black Church," *Washington Post*, July 17, 2005: B1.

28. Ibid.

6. Before and Beyond Don Imus:
On BET, Hip-Hop Culture, and Their Consequences

1. John Leo, "Imus's Enablers," *Wall Street Journal*, April 11, 2007: A14.

2. Ibid.

3. Ibid.

4. Orlando Patterson, "A Poverty of the Mind," *New York Times*, March 26, 2006.

5. Ibid.

6. Ibid.

7. Dyson made these comments on Tavis Smiley's National Public Radio show on May 27, 2004, and subsequently went on to write an entire book on the subject, *Is Bill Cosby Right? Or Has the Black Middle Class Lost Its Mind?* (New York: Basic Civitas Books, 2005).

8. William Jelani Cobb, "The Cosby Show," *The Black Commentator* 94 (June 10, 2004).

9. "Cosby Denies Second Woman's Fondling Accusation," *Associated Press*, February 9, 2005.

10. Following Smiley's release, in an unprecedented hour-long appearance on *BET Tonight* (sans Smiley), Johnson contended that Smiley's release was purely a business decision made solely by Johnson as a result of a long-running strained business relationship between the network and Smiley.

11. Ibid.

12. Milton Snoeyenbos, Robert Alemeder, and James Humber, eds., *Business Ethics* (Amherst: Prometheus Books, 1992) 33.

13. Ibid. 34.

14. Subjectivity and 'subjectivism' should not be confused. Subjectivity can be defined as personal opinions or stances that result from one's emotions or individual experiences. Subjectivism is characterized by extreme subjectivity in that one takes his or her personal experiences and opinions as definitive and absolute.

15. Ron Daniels, "The Demise of Emerge and the Ethics of Capitalism," *The Black World Today*, June 29, 2000: 2.

16. From the HSAN website, http://www.hsan.org/Content/Main.aspx?pageId=1.

17. Marie Luisa Tucker, "Where Politics and Hip Hop Collide," *Wiretap Magazine*, November 14, 2005.

18. See Paulo Freire, *Pedagogy of the Oppressed* (New York: Continuum, 1970).

7. What's Wrong with Us?
The Necessary Death of American Romanticism

1. "Obama Declares He's Running for President," CNN, February 11, 2007.

2. Horace Greeley, *The American Conflict: A History of the Great Rebellion in the United States of America, 1860–'65* (Hartford: Case, 1866) 250.

3. The Reverend James Mitchell served in this position.

4. Robert Morgan, "The Great Emancipator and the Issue of Race: Lincoln's Plan for Black Resettlement," *Journal of Historical Review* 13.5 (September/October 1993): 14; also see Benjamin Butler, *Autobiography and Personal Reminiscences of Major-General Benjamin F. Butler* (Boston: Thayer, 1892) 903–08.

5. Charles H. Wesley, "Lincoln's Plan for Colonizing the Emancipated Negroes," *Journal of Negro History* 4.1 (January 1919): 8.

6. Taylor Branch, *At Canaan's Edge: America in the King Years, 1965–1968* (New York: Simon and Schuster, 2006) 743.

7. Stanley Crouch, "What Obama Isn't: Black Like Me," *New York Daily News*, November 2, 2006.

8. Orlando Patterson, "The New Black Nativism," *Time*, February 19, 2007, 44.

9. Ibid.

10. Judy Keen, "Obama Touts Non-political Resume," *USA Today*, February 9, 2007: A1.

11. Candy Crowley and Sasha Johnson, "Is Black America Ready to Embrace Obama?" CNN, February 28, 2007.

Index